The Mainstreaming of NEW AGE

D1512143

Manuel Vasquez

11824

Pacific Press® Publishing Association
Nampa, Idaho
Oshawa, Ontario, Canada

Edited by Kenneth R. Wade
Cover art by Darryl Tank
Designed by Robert N. Mason

Dedication

I lovingly dedicate this book to

my wife Nancy

who has always believed in me and my ministry
and has truly been "the wind beneath my wings."

ISBN 0-8163-1653-8

98 99 00 01 02 • 5 4 3 2 1

Preface

Every day through the media, entertainment, and literature of all kinds, our society is being bombarded with New Age neo-pagan concepts that are, in practice and principle, diametrically opposed to biblical teachings. These ideas and philosophies that at one time seemed strange and foreign are now becoming mainstream. But what is more alarming is the fact that many of these philosophies and practices are now being embraced by church members. Like so many other Christians, Adventists are not immune to the overwhelming influence of this insidious, subtle conspiracy, which in *The Great Controversy* is referred to as "modern spiritualism" (see pages 551, 553).

Some church members, sensing that these practices and philosophies do not coincide with their Christian faith, have refused to have anything to do with them. Others have unwittingly become involved in these questionable concepts and practices, seemingly unaware of their deadly ties with the satanic, subtle New Age movement. Still others, although somewhat aware of the Eastern, non-biblical origins, take the pragmatic approach ("if it works, use it") and see nothing wrong in extracting techniques from the pagan practices, or participating in the "more acceptable" forms of New Age activity.

Actual incidences in which Adventists have become involved in the New Age, and some of the consequences, are cited in the first chapter.

This book has been written with the purpose of exposing and identifying many prevailing New Age philosophies, practices, and beliefs. As we approach the millenium, many people are seeking to satisfy their spiritual hunger with the paranormal and Eastern mysticism rather than through the Christian faith. As the populace embraces these alternative beliefs, they have become more mainstream. And because so many people defend or justify them as viable alternatives for spiritual enhancement, it is more difficult to speak out against them. But God's people must be warned because, instead of being alarmed by this paganism, many are being deceived. May God help us to recognize the danger and to see that these modern New Age beliefs and practices are deeply embedded in the occult, nurtured by the archenemy of our souls himself—Satan.

Acknowledgments

I am deeply indebted to Dr. Mervyn Maxwell, Professor Emeritus at Andrews University, who was the chair for my doctoral dissertation committee on "New Age Holistic Health: Implications for Seventh-day Adventist Faith and Practice." Dr. Maxwell went above and beyond the call of duty in working with me to complete the dissertation. He not only made many very substantial contributions to this work, but he also became deeply interested and involved in the project. I want to thank Dr. Bert Whiting, Director of the Health and Temperance Department of the General Conference, who was also a member and advisor on my doctoral dissertation committee, for his contribution and support. Will Baron is another person whom I would like to thank for his encouragement and interest in this book as well as for his expertise on the New Age, which he shared with me from time to time. I am especially thankful to my editor, Ken Wade, for his excellent editorial work and his extensive knowledge of the New Age. And lastly, I want to thank my wonderful wife, Nancy, who has worked side by side with me, putting in countless hours on the researching, typing, and editing of this book.

Contents

1. Our Overtly Neo-Pagan Society 7

2. The Big Picture 16

3. Entertainment—Discretion Advised 31

4. New Age in the Classroom 44

5. New Age Put to Music 58

6. "Wolves in Sheep's Clothing" 69

7. Eco-Feminism, Pocahontas &
   The First Angel's Message 85

8. Angels—Friends or Foes? 103

9. The Lure of New Age Holistic
   Health/Medicine 119

10. Traditional Chinese Medicine, Including
    Acupuncture 130

11. Ayurvedic Medicine, Eastern Meditation,
    and Other Occult Therapies 144

12. New Age Holistic Health Pioneers 164

13. Pragmatism: Dangerous Reasoning 170

14. Summary of New Age Holistic Health 183

15. Witnessing to the New Ager 189

16. The Last Great Deception 195

    Endnotes 201

1

Our Overtly Neo-Pagan Society

One nation under God?

Belief in the God of the Bible used to be taken for granted in America, but today in an attempt to be broad-minded, references to God have been removed from many public sites. In many cities, Nativity scenes have been banned from public property because of protests from those who take offense at government supporting any form of religious expression. Even the Girl Scouts of America, in their pledge of service, can now substitute another word or phrase for "God" that they deem more appropriate.

On any given day in America you might see, as I do on my way to work every morning, a Hindu community center, a Cambodian Buddhist Temple, or a number of other non-Christian temples or worship centers. It doesn't matter in what state you live, their presence is there.

In southern California you might see a Buddhist priest folding an American flag at one of their many temples; in South Carolina you may observe Africans worshipping their fire god; Cuban Santeria worshippers in Hialeah, Florida, may be witnessed sacrificing animals as part of their religious rituals. There are seven Buddhist temples, believe it or not, in Salt Lake City, the Mecca of Mormonism. And even the little sheltered state of Vermont, way up in the northeast, is home to a Zen monastery. Twenty-five years ago, these scenes were rare or even non-existent.

The Harvard University Pluralism Project, directed by religion professor Diana Eck, "estimates that nationwide there are 1,139 houses of worship for Muslims, 1,515 for Buddhists and 412 for Hindus."[1] The fact is that neither America nor the world has ever seen a more diverse religious nation than the United States. America now encompasses 700 to 800 "nonconventional" denominations according to J. Gordon Melton, who monitors the proliferation of religions in America for *The Encyclopedia of American Religions.* "Half of them are imported variants of standard world religions, mostly Asian; the other half are a creative and chaotic mix of U.S.-born creeds—everything from Branch Davidians to New Agers."[2]

Buddhists and Hindus have greatly influenced the way many Americans view life and death. Russell Chandler, a religion writer for the *Los Angeles Times,* in 1988 stated that "roughly 30 million Americans—about one in four—now believe in reincarnation, a key tenet of the New Age."[3] That number has no doubt dramatically increased.

It may surprise you to know that there are almost as many Buddhists in the United States as there are Seventh-day Adventists in the whole North American Division. There are 800,000 Buddhists in the US, according to a 1994 report. Some Buddhist scholars believe there are perhaps four or five times that number.[4] This should cause some concern if you take into consideration that it took the Adventist Church in America 150 years to reach that membership while the Buddhists reached that number in only a little over 30 years. These Buddhists are not all imported from the Far East either. The vast majority are "red-blooded" Americans, like Dahli Lama followers Richard Gere and Steven Segal, or perhaps one of your neighbors down the street.

Eastern religion and the New Age

If any one "religious" movement has benefited from the influx of the Eastern religious beliefs and philosophies, it has been the burgeoning New Age movement whose roots, like a tree, have drawn much of their nutrition from the Eastern mystical religions. Satan has carefully grafted this tree to bear the most alluring and forbidden fruits from all the nonChristian worldviews, beliefs, practices, and philosophies. Then he offers them to millions of his followers and unsuspecting "seekers" alike. It's a smorgasbord of irresistible, exotic morsels of beliefs and philosophies.

The New Age movement has drawn from the Hindus, Buddhists, Taoists, Native beliefs, Human Secularism, and the Occult those elements that most tantalize the human palate such as life after death, out-of-body experiences, the psychic phenomena, human potential/self-awareness, oneness with the universe, and communicating with spirit entities and nature. Thus a workable definition for the New Age movement could be "an adaptation of the philosophies, beliefs and practices of the Eastern mystical pagan religions, the occult and human secularism." It has been called "a revival of the old spiritualism" or simply, "modern spiritualism."[5]

The basic tenets of this movement are (1) no concept of sin, (2) no retribution or judgment, (3) no death, (4) no absolutes, and (5) humans are demigods (gods).

Bear in mind that not everyone who is a part of this movement practices or believes every facet of the New Age movement. Most take only what appeals to them.

Four types of involvement

There are four basic types of people that make up or become involved in the New Age movement:

1. The highly visible, open, practicing New Agers and crusaders of the New Age movement, such as actress/singer Shirley MacLaine, who is perhaps the most well known New Ager in America.

2. The closet New Agers who believe, sympathize with, and support the movement but keep a low profile, such as *Megatrends* authors John Naisbitt and his wife Aburdene.

3. Those who suspect that there are spiritual dangers involved with the New Age practices and philosophies, nevertheless feel they can select and practice certain elements from it without being affected. For example, some avail themselves of New Age Holistic

Health therapies and remedies, train in the martial arts, become involved in the popular human potential movement, or get involved with mystical meditation.

4. The unsuspecting Christians and those who get involved in the philosophies, beliefs, or practices without realizing that these are part and parcel of the New Age movement.

Adventists are not immune

Adventists are not immune to the influence of this subtle conspiracy. Consider the following examples of how some Adventists have already become entangled in the web of the New Age.

- Jenny, a loving, respectful, and obedient child became obsessed with the Nintendo video games which she received from her parents for her ninth birthday. Within six weeks, of playing Mario Brothers I and II, Zelda, and The Legend of Zelda, Jenny experienced a noticeable change of personality. Her mother sensed that Jenny was becoming possessed. "It seemed to us that she was in a trance, totally absorbed in her Nintendo and oblivious to her surroundings."
- At a supermarket on one of our university campuses, a member of the church pulls out her pendulum, holds it over the vegetables and vitamins, testing them against her allergies and whatever else may not agree with her system.
- Two academies hire a pastor known to have success locating subterranean veins of water with his divining rod to find water on their property.
- A student is expelled from two different academies because of his involvement with occult practices such as "Bloody Marys," which he learned from his girlfriend while attending public school. He has since discontinued the practice but the hologram of a witch still haunts him.
- A pastor who believes that Ellen White was a "mystic" leads workers in mystical meditation at a conference meeting and then instructs them in turn to do the same with their members during one of their 11 o'clock services.

- Students at one of our colleges interact on the Internet, participating in occult cyberspace computer games.
- A high school student "innocently" begins listening to New Age music. As she becomes hooked on its sounds and the feelings it evokes, something she didn't plan for happens. She begins seeing figures and shadows in her room at night. Sometimes her whole room lights up with a bright light. Then a heavy hand rests on her shoulder.
- A few SDA doctors on the West Coast, intrigued with Chinese acupuncture/acupressure, experiment with and incorporate these practices as alternative treatments for their patients.
- A real estate agent begins "innocently" reading her horoscope with associates at the office. Subsequently, someone suggests they visit an astrologer. Although she feels it isn't right, she goes anyway. Now she can't stay at her own house when her husband is away on business because the evil spirits won't let her alone.
- Children watching the apparently innocent "Barney" TV program learn the very first principles of pantheism as Barney occasionally puts his arms around a tree talks to it and calls it his "friend." Companion books to his TV program teach kids that they can separate their "spiritual self" from their physical bodies in innocent situations, a practice that in the occult world is called "out-of-body experiences" or "astral projections."
- A member who had been practicing iridology, reflexology, and applied kinesiology for 20 years was impressed by God to take up another line of work after reading Christian literature associating these practices with New Age holistic health. He now owns and operates a Christian bookstore.
- A Sabbath School class decides to put the Sabbath School quarterly aside and use New Age psychologist M. Scott Peck's "*The Road Less Traveled*" for the lesson study.
- A single parent is fed up with her child getting roughed up at school and decides the solution is to enroll him in an evening karate class without realizing that the oriental martial arts are inseparable from their pagan philosophies.

The New Age movement offers something for everybody—from the occult TV programming for children to Holistic Health therapies for adults. From electronic occult video games to human potential seminars. From martial arts to New Age meditative music. From imaginary conversations with spirit entities to out-of-body experiences. From horoscope readings to psychic phenomena. From the Eco-feminist Spiritualist movement and the Goddess/Wicca sects, to the animist and pantheistic views of nature that have given life and vigor to the hard-core environmentalist movement. The impact of these on our lives is intended.

Transformation

If there is one word that adequately describes the subtle New Age conspiracy, it is "transformation." The first and foremost goal of those involved in the New Age movement is to transform individuals, and eventually society. This comes through accepting a new way of thinking, a new paradigm, a new way of understanding the metaphysical and material world that leads to one's higher self, a desire for oneness with the universe, a global community, and preservation of Planet Earth. New Agers view this shift in thinking as a quantum leap forward, from a conscious awareness to an altered state of mind. From a nationalistic, parochial view of the world we live in, to a global community concept. From a Judeo-Christian value system to a neo-pagan relative value system. From absolute truth to relative truth.

Aquarian paradigm

New Agers believe that the earth moves into another astrological period roughly every 2,100 years. They say we are leaving the "Age of Pisces," which ironically began around the time of the birth of Christ and is described as a time of war, bloodshed, and injustice, and are now entering the "Age of Aquarius," supposedly an era of peace, prosperity, and harmony.

This paradigm shift involves not only a new way of looking at and understanding ourselves and the world we live in but also a "new" non-biblical spirituality. New Age spirituality is an esoteric, experiential, metaphysical, psychic awareness. It involves the belief that humans are gods, endowed with psychic abilities to communicate with the myriad disembodied spirit masters or entities in the universe—like Mozart, Newton, and Einstein, deceased world and national heroes and leaders like Mahatma Gandhi and Eleanor Roosevelt, and even biblical personalities such as John the Revelator (who is channeled by Kevin Ryerson) and Lazarus (channeled by Jack Pursel).

New Agers believe that these spirit entities desire to communicate with and impart supernatural knowledge to human beings on earth—information, for instance, about their past lives, solutions to life's problems, professional consultation on careers, and predictions about what the near future holds for them.

Modern Psychics and Astrologers

However, channelers are not the only ones that are ready and willing to reveal your past, present, and future. Modern psychics, astrologers, clairvoyants, tarot card, and I Ching readers claim to give you the insight to your future as well. Psychics and astrologers are among the most popular advisors and personal counselors today. Just watch your television for a couple hours and you will most likely see their alluring half-minute commercials or half-hour "infomercials."

The desire to know the future has intrigued people since the beginning of time—all the way back to the Garden of Eden—and is especially prominent now. The temptation to make one "wise" had this element in it. Eve perceived that the serpent knew something about her future that God would not reveal to her. And that distrust of God plunged us all into susceptibility to Satan's deceptions.

Twenty-five years ago most Americans wouldn't have been caught dead with an astrologer, a spirit medium, or a fortuneteller of any kind. But things have changed. Today many of the cinema and TV idols and even our nation's leaders openly consult them, thus giving credence and glamour to these forbidden pagan practices.

White House solarium seances

When former first lady Nancy Reagan was exposed as having consulted with Joan Quigley, the famous "San Francisco astrologer," some eyebrows were raised. When Hillary Rodham Clinton, the icon of American womanhood, stated that she had imaginary conversations with Eleanor Roosevelt to help her survive the stresses of the 1992 presidential campaign, few seemed alarmed. But someone should be.

The White House Solarium consultation and guided imagery of Hillary Clinton by her spiritual guru Dr. Jean Houston (psychic philosopher and co-director of the Foundation for Mind Research) was described in Bob Woodward's book *The Choice.* It contained detailed episodes of Hillary's "seances" or imaginary conversations with Eleanor Roosevelt, who is referred to as Hillary's "archetypal, spiritual partner."[6]

Off-limits for Christians

God's admonitions and instructions concerning involvement with astrologers, fortunetellers, and spirit mediums are very explicit. The Old Testament has several passages listing these detestable pagan practices. One of the most complete lists is found in Deuteronomy 18:9-14. It mentions the sacrificing of humans, divination, sorcery, the interpretation of omens (fortune telling), witchery, the casting of spells, mediums (channelers), or spiritists, and those who consult with the dead. That list covers a wide range of pagan and demonic practices that we Christians are not to learn, imitate, or practice in any way, shape, or form—period! When Moses rehearsed God's instructions to the Israelites as they prepared to enter the promised land, he concluded by saying, "Anyone who does these things is detestable to the Lord . . . You must be blameless (perfect) before the Lord your God. The nations you will dispossess listen to those who practice sorcery or divination. But as for you, the Lord your God has not permitted you to do so" (Deuteronomy 18:12-14).

There is no question that our society is saturated with the philosophies, beliefs, and practices of the mystical Eastern religions and the occult. Our nation is more neo-pagan oriented than Judeo-Christian. America has become a "melting pot" of Eastern pagan beliefs and philosophies. Even the media downplays and ridicules our Judeo-Christian beliefs and values. The Christian religion is often made to look ridiculous and is portrayed as outdated, fanatical, and irrelevant. In its place, the media glamorizes and promotes human secularism, mysticism, and the occult, giving people false hope and paving the way for mass deception.

Unsuspecting Christians stand to be the biggest losers in this New Age, satanically inspired conspiracy to take over the minds and allegiances of men and women, children and youth alike. The warnings of the apostle Paul to the Ephesians are a hundred times more relevant and apropos to our day. Our most ardent spiritual enemies are not physical. They are spiritual, demonic forces of the metaphysical dark realms of the evil world (Ephesians 6:10-12). How to identify and protect yourself and those you love from these insidious, subtle philosophies, beliefs, and practices of the New Age movement is the burden of this book.

2

The Big Picture

Do you like puzzles? I do. Although I haven't put one together recently, I do remember that I always started by putting together the frame, then the background. By doing this, I could get a feel for and perspective of the big picture.

The New Age movement, in some ways, is like a jigsaw puzzle with two thousand interlocking pieces. In order to appreciate the big picture, you need to be aware of its framework, foundations, and background. So let me start by putting together some of the essential pieces of the New Age framework and background.

To begin with, the New Age is a misnomer. There is nothing new about it since it is nothing more than the old spiritualism condemned by God (Deuteronomy 18:9-14; Isaiah 8:19). Satan was the instigator of spiritualism and introduced it to Eve in the orchard of her Eden home. He used the serpent to channel his first declarations on this mammoth deception. "You will not surely die . . . For God knows that when you eat of it your eyes will be opened, and you will be like God, knowing good and evil." Genesis 3:4,5, NIV.

God had said to Eve, "You will die," but Satan blatantly denied that specific divine pronouncement. "You will not surely die," he said. This was the first utterance on the deceptive teachings of spiritualism and laid the foundation for the false doctrines of the immortality of the soul, reincarnation, past lives, communicating with the dead, evil spirits, and even with Satan himself.

The serpent continued the deception by insinuating that God was keeping something good from them. "For God knows," he alleged, "that when you eat of it your eyes will be *opened*, you will *be like God*, knowing good and evil" (emphasis supplied). That was only half a truth. Their eyes were opened, but they did not become gods as promised, but rather sinners in need of a Saviour. After partaking of the forbidden fruit, they realized their finite and mortal condition more than ever. God had, in fact, been trying to keep something from them, but it wasn't anything good. It was the painful consequences of transgression. That was the knowledge that He never intended man to know.

Basic tenets of the New Age

Satan's lies to Eve that day constituted the first sermon preached on spiritualism and included the basic tenets still held today by modern spiritualism/New Age movement/New Spirituality which are:

1) No death (Immortality of the soul).
2) Mankind is divine. If divine,
3) No concept of sin, and therefore,
4) No judgment/retribution.

Six thousand years later, Ellen White, in speaking about spiritualism, confirmed that these are indeed its basic tenets: "Spiritualism declares that there is no death, no sin, no judgment, no retribution; that 'men are unfallen demigods;' that desire is the highest law; and that man is accountable only to himself."[7]

The four tenets mentioned above are based on the doctrine of the immortality of the soul. The best way of dealing with error is to present the truth. And the truth is that "the living know that they will die, but the dead know nothing; they have no further reward, and even the memory of them is forgotten. Their love, their hate and their jealousy have long since vanished; never again will they have a part in anything that happens under the sun" Ecclesiastes 9:5, 6, NIV.

Two Trees

Let's put another piece in the puzzle. There were two trees that God placed in the middle of the Garden of Eden: the tree of life, which signified life without death to those who ate of its fruit, and the tree of knowledge of good and evil. The name of the latter did not signify that the fruit of that tree could provide any and all knowledge but, rather, only the knowledge of "evil" as contrasted with "good."

And sure enough, as soon as Adam and Eve had partaken of the forbidden fruit, the Genesis account states that "the eyes of both of them were opened, and they realized they were naked" (Genesis 3:7, NIV). They had disobeyed by believing the serpent instead of God, and now they experienced guilt and shame for the first time. "So they sewed fig leaves together, and made coverings for themselves" (Genesis 3:7). The eating of the forbidden fruit by our first parents resulted in the passing on to the succeeding generations the natural bent to evil, a force, which unaided, mankind cannot resist.

Now that the framework of this New Age movement puzzle has been laid out, let me put in some of the background pieces that will bring us to the mid-1800s and modern spiritualism.

The New Age movement: Nineteenth Century roots

New Age and occult historians trace the roots of the New Age movement in America, as we know it today, to the mid-1800s, when metaphysical and spiritualistic phenomena reached a peak of popularity and "modern spiritualism" was born, a reincarnation of ancient spiritualism. The following individuals are some of the key people who prepared the way for modern spiritualism in America.

Emanuel Swedenborg (1688–1772)

The groundwork for early American modern spiritualism was laid by Swedish-born Emanuel Swedenborg, called "one of the greatest mystics of all time."[8] Swedenborg left his career as a scientist to become a mystical, religious leader and "seer" (a person with the supposed power to foretell the future), and is said to have spent the last decade of his life in intimate communion with what he claimed were angels and spirits.[9] During his pursuit of mystical experiences, Swedenborg wrote sixteen important works based solely on his "out-of-the-body experiences" and his dialogues with angels. He claimed to have had "astral tours" through the solar system and to have held converse with angels.[10] His wrestlings with evil spirits were so terrifying that his servants would flee to the farthest parts of the house for safety.[11]

Swedenborg, in states of mystical reverie, claimed "perfect inspiration." "Truths of religion," he believed, came directly from illumination.[12] He believed that the "universe was composed of several interpenetrating dimensions: the physical, mental, spiritual, angelic, and others." All are imperceptibly connected to one another. To have complete harmony in any one dimension of life depends on developing a rapport with the other levels of the cosmic scale.[13] According to Robert C. Fuller, Swedenborg taught that

> The physical body achieves inner harmony by first becoming attuned with the mind, the mind through contact with the soul, the soul through connection with superior angelic beings, and so on up the spiritual hierarchy. Through diligent study and prolonged introspection, anyone might obtain the requisite gnosis to make contact with higher spiritual planes. The benefits to be obtained were numerous: spontaneous insight into cosmological secrets; conversations with angelic beings; intuitive understanding of the hidden spiritual meaning of scripture; and the instantaneous healing of both physical and emotional disorders.[14]

These teachings were the metaphysical and spiritualistic seeds that germinated in the minds of the Theosophical Society founders Helen Blavatsky, Alice Bailey, and others. These seedlings were then nurtured by the transcendentalists like Ralph Waldo Emerson, eventually bearing fruit in the New Age movement of the 1960s and 1970s.

Franz Anton Mesmer (1733–1815)

Franz Anton Mesmer, an Austrian physician and scientist who became known as "the Father of Modern Hypnosis," was a European intellectual who greatly influenced the "modern spiritualism" movement of the mid-1800s with his so-called epoch-making discovery of a superfine fluid he called "animal magnetism," also known as "universal magnetic fluid." He claimed that this fluid resided in the entire universe and hence in everything in the world.[15] Mesmer believed that animal magnetism was also evenly distributed throughout the human body. When this animal magnetism or "mysterious life-giving energy" became deficient or out of balance, illness resulted.

Healing, however, could be restored by a person's channeling the animal magnetism from the universe. Mesmer believed that "there is only one illness and one healing."[16] A person could act as a conduit and channel the energy into other people besides himself. The energies or magnetic forces were believed to be imbued with "magical power or a healing power or a sacred spiritual energy that in the nineteenth century became known as animal magnetism, astral light, odic force, and psychic energy."[17]

Two of the major problems regarding animal magnetism in the spiritual sense were (1) that the location of this mesmeric force or fluid was uncertain. It was believed to be somewhere between the physical and the spiritual worlds; and (2) the "sensitives," or the practitioners, must possess a powerful magnetic gaze refined by concentration and self-control.[18]

Both Swedenborg and Mesmer helped to bring about the transformation from physic (the science of healing) to metaphysic (the supernatural), which "gave practitioners of unorthodox medicine a metaphysical rationale for the efficacy of their various therapeutic practices."[19]

Ralph Waldo Emerson (1803–1882)

Ralph Waldo Emerson, the "leading exponent of Transcendentalism,"[20] broke his family line of nine successive generations of ministers when he became engrossed in idealistic, transcendental philosophy. His first book, *Nature* (1836), became the Transcendentalist bible. His religious beliefs were essentially "pantheistic and syncretistic."[21] His Christ was strictly human. He advocated a faith in man, not in Christ. In his book, *Self-Reliance,* Emerson advocated a religion of "self," asserting that

> . . . the human ability to transcend the materialistic world of sense experience and facts and become conscious of the all-pervading spirit of the universe and the potentialities of human freedom. God could best be found by looking inward into one's own self, one's own soul, and from such an enlightened self-awareness would in turn come freedom of action and the ability to change one's world according to the dictates of one's ideals and conscience. Human spiritual renewal thus proceeds from the individual's intimate personal experience of his own portion of the divine "oversoul," which is present in and permeates the entire creation and all living things, and which is accessible if only a person takes the trouble to look for it.[22]

Emerson wrote, "Nothing is at last sacred but the integrity of our own mind,"[23] a belief which contains seeds of New Age thinking. He further stated: "No law can be sacred to me but that of my nature. Good and bad are but names very readily transferable to that or this; the only right is what is after my constitution; the only wrong what is against it."[24] This belief reflects the thinking in the Old Testament time of the judges, when "there was no king in Israel, but every man did that which was right in his own eyes" (Judges 17:6).

By the 1850s, popular forms of the metaphysical and spiritual phenomena had drawn from and synthesized the teachings of Swedenborg, Mesmer, and Emerson.

Among the proponents of the mid-nineteenth century metaphysical and spiritualistic movements were Helen Petrovna Blavatsky and Alice Bailey.

Helen Petrovna Blavatsky (1831–1891)

In 1875 in New York City, Helen Blavatsky, a mystic Russian

aristocrat, in company with Col. Henry Steel Olcott and William Quan Judge, founded the Theosophical Society. Their object was "to experiment practically in the occult powers of Nature, and to collect and disseminate among Christians information about the Oriental religious philosophies."[25] Madame Blavatsky had gone to India and was greatly influenced by Hindu teachings, especially reincarnation (a term which she standardized in Europe and America) and the many ascended deities. Thus "Hindu and Buddhist thought have become prominent in theosophical teaching."[26] The Theosophical Society, established in the last quarter of the nineteenth century, merged the ideas of contacting the dead and metaphysical (supernatural) healing that were part of the human race's missing knowledge.

Key elements in the theosophical beliefs are so-called "cosmic parents," "masters of wisdom," and "the ruling spiritual elite." The "ascended masters," which are also known as "spirit entities," are thought to be disembodied spirits of the world's great men and women such as the prophet Samuel, the wizard Merlin, Christopher Columbus, the Lord of the Seventh Ray, and the High Priest of Atlantis. They supposedly control the cosmos and attempt to communicate with humanity to help better human existence both materially and spiritually. Blavatsky's Theosophical Society announced "the coming of a world teacher, the Lord Maitreya, who would initiate a new cycle in human evolution—the New Age."[27] Madame Blavatsky, or HPB as she was known, "stands out as a fountainhead of modern occult thought, and was either the originator and/or popularizer of many of the ideas and terms which have a century later been assembled within the New Age movement."[28]

One of Blavatsky's students, Annie Besant, who succeeded to Blavatsky's leadership, continued developing the Theosophical Society for three decades and became an important forerunner and one of the main precursors of the New Age movement.[29]

Alice Bailey (1880–1949)

Alice Bailey, one of the leaders in the Theosophical Society, broke away because, she claimed, she was channeling masters other than the masters of Blavatsky's hierarchy. Bailey claimed to be channeling God, disembodied spirits, the collective subconscious, and even extraterrestrial entities.[30] In 1923 she and her husband, Foster Bailey, organized the "Arcane Society," which popularized the ancient practice of mediumship, or what today, in the New Age, is called "channeling."[31]

As early as 1920, Alice Bailey "introduced the idea of 'points of light' and 'light groups,' which channeled the higher spiritual forces necessary to build the New Age."[32]

The affinity that the Theosophical Society has with spiritism is that both believe in the immortality of the soul and that the disembodied spirits of the dead exist in another dimension. The Theosophical Society adherents believe that they can communicate with the ascended masters of the universe and spiritualism teaches that the living can communicate with the dead. Thus, the so-called transcendental/metaphysical spiritualism of the mid- and late-1800s was nothing more than a revival of the old spiritualism condemned in the Bible (see Deut 18:10-12).

"Modern Spiritualism" and the writings of Ellen G. White

The Great Controversy, published by Ellen G. White in 1888, makes reference to the revival of "modern spiritualism" and pegs it to 1848 and the Fox sisters. "The mysterious rapping with which *modern spiritualism* began was not the result of human trickery or cunning, but was the direct work of evil angels, who thus introduced one of the most successful of soul-destroying delusions"[33] (italics added).

The *Encyclopaedia of Occultism* concurs with this. "What is generally regarded as the birth of *modern spiritualism* took place in America in 1848. In that year an outbreak of rappings occurred in the home of the Fox family, at Hydesville, in Arcadia, Wayne County, N. Y."[34] Ellen White also stated that "the doctrine of man's consciousness in death, especially the belief that spirits of the dead return to minister to the living, has prepared the way for *modern spiritualism*"(italics added).[35]

It is no coincidence that New Age and occult historians agree with Ellen White on the beginnings of "modern spiritualism," which was the forerunner of the current New Age movement. However, since at that time these spiritualistic notions were at best "fringe" beliefs, the early American modern spiritualistic movement remained relatively small.

The Nation ripe for the New Age movement

It was not until after the counter-cultural revolution of the late 1960s and early 1970s that the philosophies and beliefs of the present New Age movement became popular. This period was unique in American history—the time of the Civil Rights movement, the flower children, Woodstock, Beatlemania, and Hare Krishnas. It was a time of bitter protest against the Vietnam War, which was viewed by many young people as an "immoral" war supported by a nation founded on Christian principles.

During 1967 and 1968 young people staged at least 204 separate demonstrations in the streets, most of them opposing America's involvement in the Vietnam War.[36] During those same years young collegiates and "hippies" (the avant-garde of a nonconventional lifestyle of mysticism, psychedelic drugs, and communal living) were questioning not only government policy but also the moral values of the status quo Christian religion. Nietzsche's criticism of Christianity was remembered: "God is Dead." Christianity had lost its meaning and relevance.

When this disenchantment with Christianity surfaced in the late 1960s and early 1970s, many young people, feeling that Christianity was dead, drab, irrelevant, and bankrupt, began looking to Eastern mystical religions for wisdom and spirituality, and this led them toward the New Age movement. One of their slogans was "Make love, not war." Ghettos like that of San Francisco's famed Haight-Ashbury district flourished across the nation. Communes patterned after Hindu "ashrams" became a way of life for many young people.

Music played a significant role in spreading the gospel of the

New Age of Aquarius and the psychedelic drug culture (free use of mind-altering, hallucinogenic drugs). Musicals like "Hair," "The Age of Aquarius," and rock stars like the Beatles from Liverpool, England, were among the leading promoters of Eastern mysticism and New Age philosophies. George Harrison's "My Sweet Lord" from his album "All Things Must Pass" was one of the first pop songs promoting homage to Hare Krishna, one of the Hindu gods. Looking back, Harrison explained,

> My idea in "My Sweet Lord," because it sounded like a "pop song," was to sneak up on them a bit. The point was to have the people not offended by "hallelu-jah" and by the time it gets to "Hare Krishna" they're already hooked, and their foot's tapping, and they're already singing along "hallelujah" to kind of lure them into a sense of false security. And then suddenly it turns into "Hare Krishna," and they will be singing that before they know what's happened.[37]

John Lennon in his song "Imagine," which is still played on light-rock stations today, articulated the aims and goals of the coming Age of Aquarius. He pictured a world where people no longer believe in heaven or hell, where there are no nationalistic divisions to cause wars, and not even religion is something to kill or die for.

Another of Lennon's songs was titled "Instant Karma." Today there are many more popular singers who also sing the phrases of the New Age philosophies, such as Elton John ("The Circle of Life"), Mariah Carey ("Hero"), Whitney Houston ("The Greatest Love"), and Vanessa Williams ("Colors of the Wind").

New Age immigration

In 1965 the Asian Exclusion Act, limiting the immigration of Indians, Chinese, and other Asians, was rescinded, allowing large-scale immigration from Eastern countries to the United States. As the immigrants came, they and their gurus brought their religious beliefs with them. Finally the time was ripe for the seeds of modern spiritualism/New Age to flourish—seeds that had been germinating since the mid-1800s. The climate of the counter-cultural revolution led many to explore and embrace the wide range of philosophies, beliefs, and practices of the New Age movement.

The phrase "New Age" has been used by its adherents and the media since the movement's outset in the late 1960s through the mid-1990s. Today, however, New Agers prefer to be identified as part of the "New Spirituality," or by their particular belief system or practice. For example, some New Age practitioners would prefer to be called "energy healers," "natural healers," or " body-soul therapists."

Goal of the New Age movement: Transformation

The New Age has as its primary objective the transformation of humanity from an old way of viewing its existence to a new way—a process referred to as a paradigm shift. New Agers promote mystical meditation, channeling, human potential, holistic health, spiritual self-awareness, and experiential, personal transformation—all in preparation for the astrological Age of Aquarius, which they believe will usher in the millennium of peace, prosperity, and harmony with the earth.[38]

One of the prominent means for accomplishing the desired transformation is healing through the methods of alternative holistic health, which is possibly the single most identifiable segment of the New Age movement.

Chapter 5 of the *New Age Almanac*, which addresses the New Age holistic health movement, states that

> transformation, as often as not, comes in the form of healing—healing of the body, mind, relationships, or the effects of spiritual traumas. Healings have often been experienced at the hands of unorthodox healing modalities and often after the failure of physicians of the more culturally accepted variety, be they medical doctors or psychiatrists. As the New Age movement developed, it accepted into itself a concurrently developing movement that was taking a new look at traditional alternative healing arts and the possibility of treating conditions with which orthodox medicine and Freudian psychiatry were

having the most difficulty. Many of these alternative medicines had a common ideological base and shared common beliefs with the New Age movement, hence their merger seemed logical.[39]

The New Age movement and Holistic Health

J. Gordon Melton, co-author of *The New Age Almanac*, notes that it was during the 1970s that

> The New Age movement and the holistic health movement merged to the extent that it is difficult, if not impossible, for an observer to draw the line between them. It is apparent that they share ideology. It is equally apparent that New Age spokespersons look to the holistic health movement as a major component of their movement, and the holistic health practitioners look to the New Agers both for public support and as the clientele upon whom they practice their profession.[40]

In 1982, America's *Megatrends* mogul, John Naisbitt, a New Age believer, wrote, "America's loss of faith in the medical establishment gave a strong symbolic push to the paradigm shift from institutional help to self-help."[41] Naisbitt forecasted this medical self-help paradigm shift in part as being from "the medical establishment's program of annual physical exams, drugs, and surgery," to a "wealth of new-age remedies—acupuncture, acupressure, vitamin therapy, charismatic faith healing, and preventive health care through diet and exercise."[42] It should be noted that New Age holistic health is a mixed bag and that Naisbitt's regimen of New Age remedies includes areas of health care that may not be specifically New Age. We certainly wouldn't dismiss things such as vitamins, diet, and exercise as New Age simply because they appear on his list.

Naisbitt's predictions have become a reality. The *New England Journal of Medicine* in January of 1993 stated that one in three Americans was using unconventional medicine.[43] *Time*'s cover story, in its November 4, 1991, issue, entitled "Why New Age Medicine Is Catching On," stated that "the growth of alternative medicine, now a $27 billion-a-year industry, is more than just an American flirtation with exotic New Age thinking. It reflects a gnawing dissatisfaction with conventional, or allopathic medicine."[44]

Russell Chandler, religion writer for the *Los Angeles Times*, in his 1988 book, *Understanding the New Age*, stated that "2%, or about 10,000, of all doctors in the United States practice some form of holistic medicine."[45]

Besides being a noninvasive and drug-free system of "wellness," alternative New Age holistic medicine emphasizes a "New Consciousness," a loose synthesis of various elements of mysticism, occultism, spiritism, and animism, combined with concepts derived from modern paranormal research (i.e., parapsychology) and from the experiences of those who have experienced altered states of consciousness.[46]

This is borne out by the burgeoning sales of pseudo-religious, parapsychology, New Age books and magazines, a large share of which are devoted to alternative medicine and holistic health. Professor and author Robert C. Fuller states that

> Most of these books, which would formerly have appeared under the now-abandoned "occult" heading, discuss such varied subjects as meditation, spirit "channeling," the mind's hidden parapsychological powers, and self-help techniques designed to help persons achieve some combination of spiritual growth and economic success. But perhaps what has most aroused public interest is the New Age movement's belief in nonmedical forms of healing. Herbal remedies, acupuncture, crystal healing, and psychic mending of the "astral body" are all being touted by the movement's adherents.[47]

Herbal remedies are also prescribed by New Age practitioners, not only because of their medicinal values, but because of their "spiritual" healing powers, as in homeopathy. The belief that each herb has a spirit is a pantheist belief. Herbology is considered a "yin" treatment and plays a central part in traditional Chinese medicine along with acupuncture to restore "balance" in the body.[48]

New Agers claim that Western medicine and health care have

lost touch with the human soul and spirit while, on the other hand, New Age medicine is bringing people back to integrating the mental, physical, and spiritual aspects of their being into the process of wellness.

It should be noted that when New Agers speak about "spiritual," it is not in reference to biblical spirituality but to a psychic self-awareness, higher self, the "god within us," and the contact with disembodied spiritual entities.

Marilyn Ferguson's book, *The Aquarian Conspiracy*, for which John Naisbitt wrote the foreword, states that this healing paradigm shift was almost effortless.

> No one had realized how vulnerable the old medical model was. Within a few short years without a shot's being fired, the concept of holistic health has been legitimized by federal and state programs, endorsed by politicians, urged and underwritten by insurance companies, co-opted in terminology (if not always in practice) by many physicians, and adopted by medical students. Consumers demand "holistic health," a whole new assortment of entrepreneurs promise it, and medical groups look for speakers to explain it.[49]

New Age alternative therapies may include carefully thought-out therapies, while other practices are based on pseudoscience, astrology, and the occult. According to Ferguson, the practitioners of New Age holistic health "include physicians and scientists with impressive credentials, chiropractors and osteopaths, psychologists and sociologists, healers and mystics, nurses and lay people as well as an odd assortment of health 'practitioners' whose ideas and techniques have varying degrees of credibility."[50]

Ferguson ties holistic health to the New Age concept of greater "self-awareness" and "transformation."

> For many Aquarian Conspirators, an involvement in health care was a major stimulus to transformation. Just as the search for self becomes a search for health, so the pursuit of health can lead to greater self-awareness.

All wholeness is the same. The proliferating holistic health centers and networks have drawn many into the consciousness movement. A nurse said, "If healing becomes a reality with you, it's a lifestyle. Altered states of consciousness accompany it, increase telepathy. It's an adventure."[51]

The New Age *Alternative Medicine: The Definitive Guide*, bearing the imprimatur of Dr. Deepak Chopra, a leading New Age Hindu author and lecturer, describes forty-three alternative therapies. The American Medical Association, in an appendix to its book *Reader's Guide to Alternative Health Methods,* lists ninety-four alternative health methods which the AMA condemns because of their purportedly non-scientific base.[52] Some of the more recognized and publicly accepted forms of New Age medicine are: acupuncture, acupressure, electropressure, applied kinesiology, aromatherapy, auriculotherapy, aura readings, ayurvedic medicine, biofeedback, chakra balancing, crystal healing, guided imagery, herbology, homeopathy, hypnosis, iridology, macrobiotic diet, pendulum divination, reflexology, reiki, rolfing, Shiatsu, therapeutic touch, and yoga.

Even though some of these treatments date back hundreds of years (to ancient traditional Chinese, Ayurvedic, and Hippocratic medicine), they, along with practices that have arisen within the last 200 years, have been embraced and made popular by the New Age movement of the 1970s because they share not only some of the same philosophies but are also viewed as vital agents of New Age transformation. "The advocates of this transformation are fond of quoting Victor Hugo's observation that 'nothing is as powerful as an idea whose time has come.' They are convinced that the time has come for a 'New Age' in medicine, for what they call *holistic health*" (italics added).[53]

3

Entertainment——Discretion Advised

Entertainment and religious values

Movies, television, and MTV are not only providing entertainment but are also forming the values, morality, and spirituality for millions in this country and the world over.

In 1997, the television networks announced that their fall line-up included an "unprecedented eight shows with religious and spiritual themes."[54] Why this sudden interest in religion or spirituality on TV? Perhaps it's because as we draw to the close of this millenium, people are seeking for spirituality, even in entertainment. "As the millenium approaches and baby boomers begin to confront their mortality, people have begun to seek out the comfort of religion in all aspects of their lives—even on TV."[55]

A recent *TV Guide* poll showed that 61% of TV viewers wanted more references to God in prime time.[56] Some new programs with religious and spiritual themes are *Good News* (a religious sitcom), *The Visitor* (mixture of religion and sci-fi), and *Nothing Sacred*, the most talked about and controversial of the three. *Nothing Sacred* revolves around a young, hip Catholic priest who struggles with his faith. Many Christian values are brought into question by one who should be defending them.

The theme of some of the other programs is "angels" and their interaction with humans, introducing unbiblical and false concepts about angel activity. In the '60s, entertainment and religion were not a good mix, but in the '90s the industry is convinced they are very compatible.

Religion and spirituality aren't all that millions of TV viewers are receiving from the "tube." They're also getting a "good" dose of New Age teachings and the paranormal as well. And this should make us sit up and take notice. You and I cannot underestimate the tremendous influence that media entertainment has on our society and, in particular, our faith. Even if you're not watching all these programs, you're still being affected because so many others are watching and being influenced. And collectively they are contributing to a shift away from biblically founded truths and norms to self-determined, spiritual pathways and values.

Chuck Colson, quoting the Christian film critic Denis Haack, said that, "It's not an exaggeration to say that Generation Xers have gained most of their worldview and values from movies and television and popular music."[57] And the cover story of *Newsweek,* July 8, 1996 stated very emphatically that "From (the movie) *Independence Day* to *The X-Files,* America is hooked on the paranormal."

Children's TV programs no exception

Children's TV programming is no exception. In fact, they are among the most blatant New Age occult and paranormal offerings on the set. Programs like *Mighty Morphin Power Rangers, Street Fighter, Mortal Kombat,* and *Savage Dragon* all contain elements of eastern and western versions of the occult. The popular "Power Rangers" are six teenagers dressed in custom-designed, form-fitting body suits, which give them a strong, high-tech look.

They are called "Morphins" because they transform themselves into Power Rangers when they receive their supernatural occult powers from the Ninjetti animal spirits: the Bear, Wolf, Crane, Frog, Ape, and Falcon. Each one calls for the power of the Ninjetti spirit power that was assigned to them by Dulcea, the Warrior Princess of the planet Phaedos. They are the "good guys" fighting the villain Ivan Ooze, his forces, and the gargoyles (grotesque human or animal creatures), using the ways of the oriental Ninja warriors.

We know that all the magic and supernatural, paranormal stuff is done with special effects, but in the dark world of the occult, many of the same things are done by demonic powers. And herein lies the serious problem. Children and teens alike, after being exposed to these programs, can develop an interest in exploring for themselves the powers of the occult world.

If you want to have a rude awakening some Monday morning, watch the USA Action Extreme Team children's programs and discover how demonic and occultic the programming has gotten. There you might see *Gargoyles*, *Sailor Moon*, and *Savage Dragon*. Their story lines involve witchery, crystal magic, mystical meditation, martial arts, fiend (evil spirit, devil, or demon) possession, sorcery of all kinds, including casting of spells.

The psalmist says, "I will set no wicked thing before mine eyes" (Psalm 101:3). And the prophet Isaiah reminds us that those who will be rewarded with eternal life will shut their eyes from seeing evil (Isaiah 33:15). Most of all, we have the instructions of God to the Israelites to keep themselves from the occult and pagan practices (Deut. 18:9-14).

Martial arts inseparable from their religious worldviews

The long-running evening TV series *Kung Fu* has also served to glorify and elevate the Chinese martial arts and Eastern mysticism. Kwai Chang Caine, the main character, employs mystical powers and magic for the sake of justice. He and his fellow sage always take the time to explain the jargon, symbolism, and Eastern philosophies that go along with their mysterious ways. Chuck Norris' TV program, *Walker, Texas Ranger,* is another one that has brought martial arts to a level of high respect and admiration. However, we cannot overlook the fact that this oriental method of bodily inflicting aggression, self-defense, physical conditioning, and enlightenment is not always what it seems to be on the surface. Martial arts are part and parcel of the Eastern philosophical, nonChristian worldviews (pantheism, monism, Taoism, etc.) which are diametrically opposed to the biblical creationist worldview.

Chuck Norris, in his book *The Secret Power Within: Zen Solutions to Real Problems*, talks about the philosophy of martial arts:

> The basic philosophy of any martial art is designed to bring you closer to yourself. That's what the dojo [where martial arts are practiced] is for: to help the student find the way to personal enlightenment. What goes on in a real dojo requires more than physical movement; it also demands mental concentration combined with a special openness. You are there to learn, and much of that learning involves discoveries that come from inside.[58]

The very first discipline of the martial arts is mystical meditation. This Eastern form of meditation is used to assist the student in achieving oneness with the universe and complete functional unity of mind, body, and spirit. Karate magazine *Black Belt* says that each time a karate student advances from one belt to another and ultimately to the black belt, it "brings the student one step closer to becoming the embodiment of the art. Each new rank contains a set of teachings which can convey the practitioner to a greater and higher self."[59]

The New Age Almanac says of the martial arts,

> Presently it is difficult to find a traditional martial arts that is not somehow associated with a religious vision of the world. . .The Chinese martial arts that have been imported into the West are frequently linked with Taoism. . .The Japanese martial arts are often associated with Zen, a form of Buddhism that exhibits strong Taoist influences.[60]

It is dangerous to think that Christians can extract the technique from the occult/pagan worldview philosophy and be safe from negative spiritual consequences. Because the martial arts incorporate Eastern philosophies and techniques, they are an easy doorway into Taoism, Zen Buddhism, and other pagan religions. As the Ninja Turtles say, "Hey, Dude, this is no cartoon," meaning this is the real thing. And we might add, spiritually dangerous as well. There are so many other sports and physical activities that do not have non-biblical worldview baggage that we can engage in.

Television sitcoms

Many of the sitcoms toy around with the Eastern religious concepts of "karma," "devas," "past lives," "ESP," "psychics," "nirvana," and "mystical meditation." The mention of these concepts and passing remarks about them by the actors are not just happenstance. They are intentional. The next time you watch your favorite sitcom, watch it with this in mind. Keep in mind also the subtle message that comes across in so much of television that there are no moral absolutes(anything goes as long as the participants are in agreement.

The truth is that New Age versions of Eastern mysticism, beliefs, and practices are in vogue. Millions have embraced them, especially the young, the "open minded," and the independent thinking educated class. New Age TV scriptwriters and producers are helping to make the paranormal attractive, acceptable, and mainstream.

The powerful influence of the movies

Films are among the greatest mind changers of all time. For example, even though most Americans, in theory, disapprove of adultery, after viewing the movie *Bridges of Madison County*, a film that celebrated adultery, millions were moved with compassion for the unfaithful farmer's wife, Francesca, (played by Meryl Streep). In fact, one poll showed that nearly half the moviegoers that saw the film thought that Francesca should have run away with her lover Robert Kincaid, played by Clint Eastwood.

Movies have a powerful influence on the viewer because they seem so real. The well-written script, the sentimental music track, the laid-back, secluded setting, the two top actors helped to justify people's thinking that this adulterous relationship between Francesca and Kincaid was a "good thing." You and I can't afford to underestimate the influence the cinema has on our thinking. Today's films are not only creating new moral standards, they are questioning the very existence of God, the nature of man, teaching that we are divine, never dying, always reincarnating. Movies have become the "cat-echisms" for the occult and Eastern religious philosophies.

Introducing Buddhism to millions

Films like *Little Buddha, Seven Years in Tibet,* and *Kundun,* have also taught westerners the ways of Buddhism. *Little Buddha* is the story of Buddhist monks in search of the reincarnation of Buddha. Their search leads them to Jesse, an 8-year old American boy living in Seattle. In the process of convincing Jesse's parents to allow him to go to Tibet with them, Jesse, along with all the other millions of viewers, is taught all about the mystical beliefs of Buddhism.

Brad Pitt, one of the hottest male stars in Hollywood, gives an academy-award winning performance in the Buddhist film *Seven Years in Tibet.* Here again is a classic example of a Westerner, this time a European, being immersed in the Buddhist culture and com-ing to see the world through the nonbiblical worldview of Buddhism. Brad Pitt tries to construct a building and finds himself in a di-lemma. His workers will not dig the foundation because they refuse to kill any worms. The reason? Because, they explain, one of the earthworms in a past life could have been his mother. Does this sound familiar? You guessed it. Buddhists believe in the transmigra-tion of lives, which includes all forms of life, even worms.

Kundun is the impressive story of the celebrated Dalai Lama, the exiled Buddhist spiritual leader of Tibet, mainly seen through his eyes. The Dalai Lama has become the "poster guru" of Holly-wood, mainly through the efforts of devoted followers like Richard Gere, Steven Segal, and Harrison Ford. By the way, it was Melissa Mathison, Harrison Ford's wife, who wrote the movie script for *Kundun.* Another interesting note is that in February of 1997Hollywood's action hero, Steven Segal, "was recognized by the head of the venerable Nyingma Tibetan lineage as the reincarnation of a fifteenth-century lama."[61]

Other celebrities boosting Buddhism in the media are punk-rap Beastie Boys singer, Adam Yauch. Yauch converted to Buddhism in 1992 and has organized the Tibetan Freedom concerts. Tina Turner the rock-n-roll "diva", recites Soka Gakkai Japanese Buddhist chants as part of her spiritual rituals.[62] Hollywood stars that are followers and admirers of the Dalai Lama are too many to mention. Hollywood's hype on Buddhism has definitely contributed to the nearly one million Americans who are Buddhists or who believe and practice certain aspects of Buddhism.

New Age sci-fi occultism is another theme that is being glamorized on the silver screen. No one has done this so well as two of Hollywood's giant film producers, George Lucas and Steven Spielberg. Let's take a closer look at a classic example of New Age sci-fi movies—the *Star Wars* Trilogy.

George Lucas' *Star Wars* — an American classic

"A long time ago in a galaxy far, far away . . ." was the enticing way in which film producer George Lucas began *Star Wars*, his first "blockbuster" science fiction movie, which was laced with New Age philosophies and beliefs. It won seven Oscars and was quickly followed by *The Empire Strikes Back* and *The Return of the Jedi* to complete the tremendously popular *Star Wars* trilogy. *Star Wars* was one of those films that every teenage boy wanted to see a dozen times. With tens of millions of fans, it has earned its place as an American family classic. *Star Wars* was listed as one of the all-time box office hits, totaling millions at the box office, not to mention all the other revenues that were realized through the sale of novels, toys, costumes, books, TV programs, video games, comic books, and records.

At its twentieth anniversary, George Lucas' new release of the same trilogy, *Star Wars*, with the latest up-to-date technology added, made it an even greater all-time box office classic. The baby boomers who were first thrilled with *Star Wars* are now introducing their own children to the new technologically enhanced version of the outer space adventures of Luke Skywalker, Leia Organa, and Darth Vader.

Star Wars—another worldview

Why the fascination with *Star Wars* and other films like it? One reason is that science fiction has always intrigued a large segment of society. People wonder about life on other planets and whatever else is out there beyond our solar system. They have come to trust science sometimes more than they trust the Bible. The fiction aspect of *Star Wars* has given the viewers another worldview option: a pantheistic Taoist philosophy of a so-called "universal force" that permeates the universe and everything in it. This is in opposition to the biblical teachings of a personal God who created, sustains, and controls the universe—a personal, supernatural being with a moral, ethical code binding on humans.

The Plot

The plot is the old-time standard of the war between good and evil. The Old Republic is about to fall to the Dark Forces. Princess Leia, the surviving Jedis, and The Alliance are in hiding. Just before her capture, Leia sends a message through a droid (R2-D2) to Obi-Wan "Ben" Kenobi, one of the old, yet most prominent Jedi Knights who is living on the planet of Tatooine.

Luke Skywalker, adopted and raised by Owen and Beru Lars on the planet Tatooine, is suddenly drawn into the struggle of the Alliance against the Dark Forces. Skywalker, who trains to become a Jedi, is taught to fight in the ways of the Force by Ben Kenobi. Ben had trained Luke's father, Anakin Skywalker, before Anakin was corrupted and seduced by the dark forces and later became known as the dreaded Darth Vader. Luke was also trained by Yoda, an 800-year old diminutive creature. In the end, Darth Vader is converted to the good side of the force by saving his son Luke from destruction by the evil Emperor Palpatine. Darth Vader lifts Palpatine up and throws him into the shaft of the power core. Luke then restores the ancient order of the Jedi and provides hope for the future of the good side of the force.

The Subtle Agenda

Star Wars did more than just entertain millions. It introduced them to the pantheistic Taoist worldview philosophy of a universal energy referred to as "the force." According to Obi-wan Kenobi,

"The Force is what gives the Jedi his power . . . It is an energy field created by all living things. It surrounds us and penetrates us; it binds the galaxy together." Throughout the trilogy, the most-recalled phrase that stayed with the viewers was "May the Force be with you."

Luke Skywalker (as well as the millions of viewers) was taught by Obi-Wan Kenobi and Yoda the arts of levitation, visualization, clairvoyancy, ESP, and telekinesis. These concepts are elements embraced and taught by the New Age segment of parapsychology and metaphysical phenomena. Through the cinema, Satan packages the occult elements of the New Age in interesting, exciting, and subtle ways. In this way, millions are indoctrinated to modern spiritualism/New Age.

George Lucas influenced by Joseph Campbell

Perhaps we should look at the man behind this tremendously popular outer space trilogy. George Lucas, who grew up in Modesto, California, from a very early age nurtured his mind with comic books and Saturday morning cartoons.[63] Later, he became concerned about the way people were learning their mythology from TV programs. He felt it made them confused because there was no point of view or sense of morality in them. So he said he developed *Star Wars* as a means of helping kids become morally anchored.[64] But in doing so, he introduced his audiences to the mysticism and metaphysical world of science fiction.

When asked if *Star Wars* was a morality play, Lucas replied:

It's also a psychological tool that children can use to understand the world better [worldview] and their place in it and how to adjust to that. It's very basic. It's where religion came from. Fairy tales, religion, were all designed to teach man the right way to live and give him a moral anchor."[65]

Some of George Lucas' inspiration for *Star Wars* came from his extensive reading of the works of Joseph Campbell, the well-known mythology and philosophy professor of the twentieth century. Lucas' notion of "the Force," which turned out to be the most powerful concept that people remembered from the film, was derived from Campbell's writings.[66] In an interview with Campbell, Bill Moyer, an acclaimed television journalist, posed a question about a higher cause. Campbell replied,

> I would say, a more inward cause. "Higher" is just up there, and there is no "up there." We know that. That old man up there has been blown away. You've got to find the Force inside you. This is why Oriental gurus are so convincing to young people today. They say, "It is in you. Go and find it."[67]

The authors of Joseph Campbell's life story, Stephen and Robin Larsen, claim that "the concepts that most fascinated Campbell probably originated more with Freud's Swiss colleague, Carl G. Jung."[68] So some of the mythological and metaphysical concepts that came from Carl Jung and flowed through Campbell finally materialized in some of George Lucas' movie creations.

The gospel according to "Saint Lucas"

The Christian parallels in the *Star Wars* trilogy are worthy of note. For instance, Darth Vader, like Lucifer, was corrupted when he sought power. Once a Jedi Knight, he turned from the good side and joined the Dark force of the universe to become one of the most dreaded commanders of the Evil Empire. Like Satan, he was the one who was constantly tempting Luke Skywalker to join the Dark side by offering him a share of the Empire. But unlike the devil, Vader in *The Return of the Jedi* has a change of heart at the end and instead of destroying Skywalker, who turns out to be his son, he destroys Emperor Palatine, the epitome of Darkness, by casting him down the shaft of the power core. In this way, he redeemed himself and earned a place with Yoda and Obi-Wan Kenobi, among the elite disembodied spirits to lead Luke in the ways of the Force. But it was not as Darth Vader, but as Luke's father, Anakin Skywalker that he did this.

Luke Skywalker takes on the role of the Christian, struggling within himself while fighting evil without. He is also like the New Age spiritual seeker who is trying to find his path. Skywalker must learn to use the force in fighting the powers of evil. But unlike a Christian, Luke used occult powers like mental telepathy with his sister, Princess Leia, when they were separated and he was in danger; he practiced telekinesis (moving objects with the mind) when drawing his light saber to himself and when moving rocks; he used levitation when fighting with Darth Vader—all of which were taught to him by Kenobi and Yoda.

Han Solo is the equivalent of a modern skeptic who does not put his trust or faith in religious, supernatural things. He, like so many human secularists, placed his trust in himself. His philosophy was "Hocus-pocus religions and archaic weapons are no substitute for a good blaster at your side."[69] He was the wisecracking, smart-alecky mercenary who lived "by the seat of his pants," and who without really trying, became a hero.

In Lucas' trilogy, Yoda is the guru or spiritual master. Yoda, who only taught the most serious of students, taught Luke to meditate for long periods of time and to levitate objects. He also made his students "unlearn that which their upbringings, and their own eyes and ears, had taught them."[70] "Forget your old measures. Unlearn, unlearn!" he told Luke. "Luke truly felt ready to unlearn all his old ways and willing to free himself to learn all this Jedi Master had to teach."[71] Yoda taught his students "that affinity with nature enhanced an affinity with the Force."[72] Yoda was to Luke Skywalker what Miaggi was to Daniel in *Karate Kid* and its sequels—an Eastern mystical sage and mentor.

Steven Spielberg's New Age movies

George Lucas's long-time friend, Steven Spielberg, is the other movie producer who has contributed to the popularity of New Age sci-fi and Eastern mystical beliefs through his movies: all-time box office favorites such as *Close Encounters of the Third Kind, E.T., Always, Raiders of the Lost Ark,* and *Indiana Jones and the Temple of Doom.* All made their indelible mark in the minds of countless millions.

Indiana Jones and the Temple of Doom was the story of a poor village somewhere in India. When Indiana Jones, played by Harrison Ford, gets there, he finds the people languishing and disheartened. The crops have failed. Their idol, the Shankara stone (the image of Shiva's phallus or male organ), and their children have been taken away by a Tantric sect. Tantra worshipers believe that sexual experiences can open the hidden (occult) dimensions of psychic powers within ourselves. They also believe that the ultimate masculine (Shiva) and feminine (Shakti) creative energies that created the entire cosmos, lie within us. That's why, with the sacred stone taken away, life was diminishing for them. Something had to be done or they would all die.

In this film, Indiana Jones decides to rescue both the children and the sacred stone. In doing so, the script introduces the tantric Hindu worship of the Shiva Lingam or the god Shiva's phallus.

When I went to Varanasi (Old Banares), India, I visited the temple of Kali (the goddess who rides on a snake and desires blood). There I saw a shrine to the Shiva Lingam. It was a huge concrete or granite stone image of Lord Shiva's Lingam/phallus protruding from his consort's female organ (which is called *yoni*). I saw where barren women had poured milk all over Shiva's phallus and worshiped it so that Shiva would impregnate them. If and when they bore a child, they would come back to pay their vows. Also, I have discovered that Bisheswar, another name for Shiva, who is depicted as a "lingam" is the reigning deity of the city.[73]

Vishal Mangalwadi, who was born and raised in India and has seen and studied the New Age firsthand, writes in his book *When the New Age Gets Old*,

> The idea that we can have spiritual experience through sex was introduced to millions of people through the 1984 thriller movie *Indiana Jones and the Lost Temple of Doom*. The hero rescues the "Shankara stone" from a tantric sect to deliver it to its rightful possessors. The Shankara stone is "Shiva-lingam" (i.e., the god Shiva's phallus), more worshiped than understood by Hindus. In the movie, the villains had found three primeval Shiva-lingams, and were searching for the other two so as to unite them with Kali (Shakti), the female consort of Shiva.[74]

Today's movies are tremendously entertaining. Millions of dollars are spent filming them—$28 million for *Indiana Jones and the Temple of Doom.* But remember, while you are sitting there being entertained with all this adventure, suspense, and intrigue, Satan is subtly displacing truth with error. Seeds of doubt are sown. Alternative worldviews and religious philosophies are introduced which can erode your faith. It doesn't happen overnight. But it does happen, gradually.

The watchword—discretion advised

> It is a law both of the intellectual and the spiritual nature that by beholding we become changed. The mind gradually adapts itself to the subjects upon which it is allowed to dwell. It becomes assimilated to that which it is accustomed to love and reverence.[75]

So much could be said about the scores of other films, including many of those produced by the Walt Disney Film Industry. Walt Disney, or José Luis Girao, his birth name, was born in Almeria, Spain, and came to the United States with his parents when he was just a boy. When his parents died, José Luis was adopted by Elias Disney, who then changed his name to Walt. Were Disney alive today, he would be shocked at what has happened to the good, wholesome family entertainment empire he built.

The battle for the mind between good and evil has increased a hundredfold. Satan knows that he has precious time left before it's all over and the destiny of all the living will be sealed. It matters little to him whether you get into the metaphysical, paranormal, Wicca, psychic phenomena, martial arts, past lives, Eastern mysticism, yoga, mystical meditation, or New Age holistic health, as long as he sidetracks you from the truth and your Saviour. Therefore, when choosing your entertainment, the watchword should be "discretion advised."

4

New Age in the Classroom

What I learned in school today

"What did you learn in school today?" used to be the most natural question you would ask your grade-school child when he or she came home from school. Today, the question may be the same, but the answers may shock you. If parents could sit in many of the modern classrooms today, they would be alarmed to find out what their children are being taught by some of their teachers. It's becoming commonplace to hear that Judy or Joey talked to a "spirit guide" or an angel during their rest period. Or that allegiance to the flag and our country are not important or even necessary any more. Or that the children are the only ones responsible for forming their value system of what is right and wrong.

One Sabbath morning as I was waiting in the pastor's study to go on the platform to speak, the lady who was going to give the scripture reading said to me, "Can you tell me what to say to my little girl?"

"Why?" I asked her.

"Well, she came home from school this week telling me that she doesn't believe in God like I do anymore. My daughter was told by one of her teachers that 'Satan is as good as God,' and that's what she said she believed."

"How old is your daughter?" I asked.

"She's seven."

Wow, I thought to myself, *Seven years old and already challenging the religious beliefs her mother taught her.*

In the very brief time we had before we went on the platform, I told her that she should sit down with her daughter and on a piece of paper put the words "God" on the left-hand side and "Satan" on the right-hand side. Then list under God's name all the good things He has done and list all the evil things that Satan has done under his name, beginning with his rebellion in heaven. "Go over each one, showing your daughter that God is loving, good, and has our best interests at heart. And that Satan is evil, deceiving, and out to destroy us. Appeal to her mind as well as her heart," I told her.

On another Sabbath, after I had given an afternoon lecture on New Age in the classroom, another concerned mother came up to me and said, "Now I understand what my first-grader was trying to tell me when she came home from school saying that she had talked to Jesus. At first I didn't know what to make of it, so I just passed it off as unimportant. But now it's making sense to me. Her teacher was doing guided imagery with the class, teaching them to visualize Jesus and have 'imaginary' conversations with Him."

New Age in the classroom

New Age is no longer something out there in a small segment of society. It has gone mainstream and in the last decade, it has come into the classroom at all levels. The most important facet of the New Age movement is education. And for good reason. New Agers know that in order to create a new world society for the new millenium, the Age of Aquarius, they must start with the children in their formative years of learning. The youngsters, they feel, need to develop a planetary and global consciousness at the very outset of their lives.

New Age advocate, Marilyn Ferguson, wrote in her New Age manifesto, *The Aquarian Conspiracy* that "You can only have a new society, the visionaries have said, if you change the education of the younger generation."[76]

This sounds a little like the biblical philosophy to "Train a child in the way he should go, and when he is old he will not depart from it." (Proverbs 22:6). Every philosophical ideology or genius understands this. Hitler knew it. The Communists knew it. The New Agers know it—and they have tremendously influenced the educational curriculum with their philosophies to implement the new paradigm shift of understanding the world and the universe we live in.

New Age concepts being taught

Thus thousands of classrooms around the country and the world are becoming transformation learning centers for the twenty-first century generation of New Agers. The conspirators, as Marilyn Ferguson refers to the New Agers, are busy introducing psychotherapeutic techniques and occult practices in programs such as "Pumsy," "Quest" and "DUSO." These programs incorporate learning modalities or concepts such as:

1. holistic education
2. transpersonal education
3. global education
4. humanistic psychology
5. values clarification and situational ethics
6. relativism
7. meditation, visualization techniques, and guided imagery

It was not surprising, therefore, to learn that, according to the Aquarian Conspirators' survey conducted by Ferguson, educators such as teachers, administrators, policymakers, and educational psychologists were involved in the New Age more than any other single category.[77]

If you stop to think of the time our children spend in the classroom—7 hours a day, 180 days per year—many times at the feet of a New Age educator or a naïve teacher who thinks these New Age concepts of teaching floating around are novel and effective, this should alarm you.

Granted, most of these New Age concepts of learning are being taught in the public schools. But we can't be too overconfident that some of these concepts aren't being taught in our church schools as well. The problem is that since the New Age continues to evolve, it is hard to define. Even New Agers disagree on what is and what is not New Age. So, not always being able to define the New Age, the enemy, has been one of the greatest strategies Satan has come up with. Because of this, many sincere Christians are also caught up in this web and are totally unaware of its spiritual dangers.

New Age concepts are never labeled as such. Instead, they are disguised by words and phrases such as those in the list above. Still others are more deceiving such as: self-esteem, self-enhancement, self-reliance, potential discovery, centering, meditation, and creating your own reality. All sound pretty innocent until you realize where they originated. Also bear in mind that the occult, which is part of the New Age, has changed its outward appearance for the masses. It has a new and modern appeal. No longer is it found in dark, spooky rooms. Today the occult is out in the sunlight, promising all the good things of life such as love, joy, peace, wisdom, and self-awareness.

Marilyn Ferguson, who dedicated a 42-page chapter ("Flying and Seeing: New Ways to Learn") to the subject of education in her 1980 *Aquarian Conspiracy* book says that:

> Subtle forces are at work, factors you are not likely to see in banner headlines. For example, tens of thousands of classroom teachers, educational consultants and psychologists, counselors, administrators, researchers, and faculty members in colleges of education have been among the millions engaged in *personal transformation*.[78]

"Subtle forces" working for the "personal transformation" of our educators is significant. And once they are "transformed" to the new paradigm of education, they are committed to implementing it in their classrooms. "Transformed educators," as they are called, see no problem in using, for example; altered states of consciousness, self-hypnosis, meditation, and other occult practices. Under the subtitle "The New Curriculum," Ferguson writes:

> Altered states of consciousness are taken seriously: "centering" exercises, meditation, relaxation, and fantasy are used to keep the intuitive pathways open and the

whole brain learning. Students are encouraged to "tune
in," imagine, the special feeling of peak experiences. There
are techniques to encourage body awareness: breathing,
relaxation, yoga, movement, biofeedback.[79]

All these consciousness-expanding occult New Age techniques are
used deliberately in tens of thousands of classrooms around the world
by transformed teachers with a very definite purpose. Ms. Ferguson
does not conceal this fact, rather she takes pride in declaring it. "The
deliberate use of consciousness-expanding techniques in education, only
recently well under way, is new in mass schooling."[80]

The added emphasis of consciousness-expanding techniques in
modern education to guide students into altered states of consciousness and into the metaphysical spirit world is dangerous. The argu-
ment that to become better learners or successes in life students need
to employ altered states of consciousness is a myth, an insidious
misconception inspired by Satan himself. There is a design and a
designer behind all this madness, a demonic, subtle conspiracy taking place that we don't always understand. For the New Ager, this
may be a new, exciting way to success. But for the Christian, there is
a better way—God's way. The psalmist said it: "The fear of the Lord
is the beginning of wisdom." (Psalm 111:10).

Perhaps at this point we should take a closer look at some New
Age concepts being taught in the classroom today:

Holistic Education
1. Holistic Education, which is a philosophy of education that
takes into account the whole person, is also shared by the Seventh-
day Adventists. Ellen White states that true education "is the harmonious development of the physical, the mental, and the spiritual
powers."[81] However, New Age holistic education is not to be confused with the wholistic education of the Seventh-day Adventist
Church. The big difference lies in the third dimension, the spiritual. For the church, it refers to the biblical concept of spirituality.
In the New Age, it refers to the psychic powers and metaphysical
experience.

Transpersonal Education

2. Transpersonal (beyond the person) education proposes to help the student develop his or her "full potential." In order to accomplish this, it employs various forms of Eastern and occult beliefs and techniques.[82] Ferguson, in her book, *The Aquarian Conspiracy*, gives us a New Age perspective of transpersonal education.

> The name derives from a branch of psychology that focuses on the transcendent capacities of human beings. In transpersonal education, the learner is encouraged to be awake and autonomous, to question, to explore all the corners and crevices of conscious experience, to seek meaning, to test outer limits, to check out frontiers and depths of self.

Its aims, she stated are

> . . . for a new kind of learner and a new kind of society. . . Transpersonal education is more humane than traditional education and more intellectually rigorous than many alternatives in the past. It aims to aid transcendence, not furnish mere coping skills. It is education's counterpart to holistic medicine: education of the whole person.[83]

Transpersonal education's aims are clearly stated: they are to aid in transcendence not for "mere coping skills."

Secular Humanism

3. The secular humanism approach to education employs such tools as values clarification, situational ethics, and psychotherapeutic techniques. Secular humanism also teaches that humans don't need God. They can do it all on their own. And that every phenomenon can be explained through science or logic.

Values Clarification

4. In the "values clarification" concept, there are no absolutes. Everything is relative, personal, or situational. The students are taught to take charge of their own lives and justify their values and conduct.

They determine what is right and wrong for themselves. It's no wonder many of our public schools have to install high-tech security systems and have police walking the halls.

The problem with this New Age concept is that the individual student becomes the only source from which to draw and make this kind of lasting, moral judgment. Others have no say in the matter. And that is unfortunate. By contrast, Christians are admonished to seek wisdom and knowledge from the Lord, to value the instruction of godly parents, to base their moral values on the "thus saith the Lord" and not on what we think. For we are not our own. We belong to God our Maker, and He has already given us a set of moral values called the Ten Commandments. Any conduct that goes against His laws is rebellion, plain and simple.

The Scriptures clearly state that: "The heart is deceitful above all things, and desperately wicked: who can know it?" (Jer. 17:9). Jesus said that it is out of the heart that "proceed evil thoughts, murders, adulteries, fornications, thefts, false witness, blasphemies" Matt 15:19. So if we look inward, all we will find is evil and wickedness, not wisdom and goodness. The only right source for one's values is God's Holy Word.

Globalism

5. Global education teaches that global loyalty is the all-important thing. No more loyalties to a particular country or allegiance to a flag. Just one happy global community. As John Lennon sings in his song "Imagine:" "And the world will be as one." In order to achieve a global community with one economy, one monetary system, one government, and one religion, globalists feel that there must be a values clarification, relativism tolerance. In this sense global education has become the political side of the New Age movement in the world.

The New Age globalist logic goes something like this:

In the future we will be faced with many situations in which we will need to promote harmony and cooperation. Since this is needed for survival in the global village, we must abandon the separatist notion of absolutes. Absolutes lock us into conflict-oriented relationships and do not allow for compromise. Acceptance of ambiguity will be a valued attitude for future generations.[84]

The opposite of globalism is ethnocentrism. "Ethnocentrism" means you're loyal to your own ethnicity, country, flag, and culture. This is the way the world has operated for centuries. New Age globalists believe that this earth will become their utopia in the emerging Age of Aquarius. On the other hand, we Christians believe that our utopia will begin when Christ returns the second time to take the redeemed to live with Him in heaven (John 14:1-3; 1 Thess. 4:17).

What global education really does is crowd the study of the Christian's worldview and Western civilization out of the student's curriculum. For instance, the teacher will illustrate the global interdependence by a "chocolate candy bar." A worksheet is then handed out showing that the ingredients of the bar came from all over the world. Global education also tends to promote the Eastern religions over Christianity.

Eric Buehrer, in his book *The New Age Masquerade*, tells of a little third-grade girl from a small town in Wisconsin who had put in a lot of time working on a Valentine's card. When she finished her "masterpiece" and handed it to her teacher with satisfaction and pride, the teacher took one look at it and handed it back. Then she told the little girl to make it over. "Why?" she asked. The teacher answered, "You wrote 'I Love Jesus' at the top and that phrase cannot be displayed alongside the other kids' cards because it's offensive. This is a public school."[85]

But I wonder, as Buehrer did, "What if a Hindu child would have put a Hindu sankrit phrase like "Om" on her card. Or what if a Buddhist student would have put a Yin Yang symbol on his Valentine's card. If the teacher would have seen this, she might have taken it as an opportunity for "classroom cultural enrichment."

Advocates of New Age education

Some of the names pushing The New Age agenda for education are Jack Canfield, Thomas Roberts, Barbara Clark, Deborah Rozman, Maureen Mardock, Gay Hendricks, Jean Houston, and David B.

Ellis, all of whom have written on the subject.

Jack Canfield

Jack Canfield is the director of Educational Services for Insight Training Seminars in Santa Monica, California. He is a founder and past director of the Institute for Holistic Education in Amherst, Massachusetts. And yes, the author and co-author of all those *Chicken Soup for the Soul* books. John Ankerberg and John Weldon in their book *Encyclopedia of New Age Beliefs* state that in one of Canfield's self-esteem newsletters, he and Paula Klimeck discussed the importance of transpersonal education.

> Almost the entire gamut of the occult is endorsed as being applicable to children's education, including dream work, mandalas, meditation, arica psychocalisthenics, yoga, occult "centering," "sacred" dances such as those found at the spiritistic Findhorn community in Scotland, and the anthroposophical eurythmy/sufi dances, teaching children to psychically see their chakras, auras, and healing energies, magic circles, and psychic chanting.[86]

Canfield on one occasion used the popular TV series of *Kung Fu* to aid a group of sixth graders in contacting their personal "inner guides." By reflecting on what Caine, the hero, did every time he was in a serious predicament, the students realized that just by closing his eyes and meditating, Caine could flash back to a time when his teacher had told him something wise and important and thereby find a solution to his problem.

> I then asked them what kind of teacher Caine talked to. Was he like their sixth-grade teacher? They all agreed that he was a different kind of teacher, somehow more special, more wise and more able to be trusted. They all agreed they would like to have a teacher like that.[87]

Canfield asked them if they would like to have a wise old teacher whom they could get help from in times of trouble. They all said Yes but didn't know where they could find one. They thought they'd have to go to China, Japan, or India. Canfield told them they could try to find a wise person inside themselves. The kids were then encouraged to close their eyes, take a few deep breaths, and were led, through visualization exercises, to contact their own spirit guides.[88] Canfield told them:

"You are about to meet a special guide, your own special guide . . . Let whatever happens happen . . . Communicate with your guide in whatever way possible . . . Listen to your guide."[89]

Jean Houston

Jean Houston, a human potential guru and the lady who taught Hilary Rodham Clinton to have "imaginary conversations" with Eleanor Roosevelt and Mahatma Gandhi, has also made an impact on educational learning. In her book *Mind Games*, which is a how-to book on achieving altered states of consciousness without the use of drugs, she recommends, "meditation and visualization techniques which can lead the practitioner to a 'new image of man as a creature of enormous and unfolding potentials.' "[90]

Jean Houston has been a personal friend and consultant to at least two of the families in the White House: the Carters and the Clintons. In September 1979, she held a conference entitled "Policy Alternatives for the Decade Ahead" for several hundred government officers at an inn in Easton, Maryland. The purpose was to explore means to better society as well as the people in it. What she did with all those heads of national agencies, undersecretaries, assistant secretaries of government departments, and representatives from the White House was unprecedented, to say the least. She put most of them in a hypnotic trace and did "guided imagery" with them. She described the scene this way:

> Before me, stretched out on the floor of an inn in Easton, Maryland, are several hundred government officials. I have put most of them in a trance and am guiding them to travel to a future "possible society" and bring back descriptions of what they find there.[91]

Why is Houston into all this occult business? Because she believes that the New Age notion of the imminent planet-wide transformation of the human race is at hand. She said that "humankind is finally at the crossroads of this transformation which makes this a challenging and exciting time."[92]

David Ellis

David Ellis wrote the college textbook *Becoming A Master Student*, which was used to help freshman students succeed in college. It employed several occult New Age memory techniques. For instance, exercise #11 is called "A Little Self-Hypnotism," describing how the student can do autohypnosis.

> Close your eyes or focus on a point several feet away. Take three slow, deep breaths, pay attention to each breath. Then take three more breaths while consciously relaxing your entire body. Once your mind is relaxed and your mind is stilled, say to yourself, "At any time I choose, I will be able to recall. . ." Insert a brief description of what you want to remember at the end of the sentence. Repeat the entire exercise three times.[93]

In another section of Ellis' book, he recommends "Meditation and How to Do It" as a deeper way of relaxation than sleep. He introduces it from a Hindu perspective: "The word 'meditate' came from the sanskrit word *medha* which means literally, 'locating your center, your inner wisdom.' Meditation is now being taught and endorsed by everyone from gurus in long, white gowns to medical doctors."

Ellis offers the following five guidelines for meditation:
1. "Make a commitment."
2. "Set a specific time."
3. "Pay close attention to your breathing."

> Sit in a comfortable position with your spine erect. Notice your breath as it flows gently in and out of your body. *Imagine* yourself breathing in calmness, relaxation, and well-being. *Visualize* yourself breathing out frustrations, tensions and negative emotions (italics added).[94]

The practice of imagining and visualizing your breathing in and out is strictly an Eastern form of inducing an altered state of consciousness.

4. "Clear your mind." Here the instructions are:

Concentrate on something to lessen distractions.

Repeat silently a word or a phrase (love, God, yes, om) or stare at a candle flame.

Allow your mind to go blank. Each time a thought enters, gently let go.

Another thought will soon enter; let it float away.[95]

Here are at least three overt red flags.

- Repeating the word *om*—"In Hinduism, the most sacred and comprehensive expression of spiritual knowledge."[96]
- Staring at a candle flame is a method used by many followers of Hinduism, Buddhism, and New Agers, such as Shirley MacLaine. She stares at a flame until she hypnotizes herself.
- Allowing your mind to go blank, which is another element of Eastern meditation.

5. "Consider Taking a Class." And here the suggestion is:

"Local meditation centers, YMCA's, and community education programs teach a wide variety of meditation styles. You can learn meditation that involves movement (tai chi), breathing and postures (yoga), or science and ceremony (transcendental meditation)."[97]

I believe that all of these should be considered off limits for sincere Christians.

This is a sample of some of the blatant New Age occult practices being taught to college students in this textbook. There are fifty-six exercises easily located by their blue circle image containing a lady in a meditative lotus position. Even though many of these elements which are offensive to Christians were removed in the 6th edition, the entire textbook is still saturated with New Age philosophy for developing memory potential.

These are just a few of the bright people that are bringing New Age into the classroom. Most of these are self-declared New Agers or at least human potential leaders who have embraced Eastern worldview philosophies. The question now is "What about Christian education? Is it the same?" The answer is No. The reason is that we have a biblical, theist worldview philosophy that is worlds apart, as far as the East is from the West.

Praise God for Christian education

The Seventh-day Adventist Church worldwide operates 5,455 church schools, including schools of higher learning. It employs tens of thousands of dedicated, God-fearing teachers who not only dispense book knowledge but realize that they have the awesome responsibility of molding the minds and characters of their students according to God's will. These are the unsung heroes of the Adventist Church who have helped prepare their students to become church leaders as well as faithful members of God's church.

I think of all the wonderful, great, and godly teachers I have had the privilege of studying under at Union College, Loma Linda University, and Andrews University. There are too many to name, but these men and women left an indelible, lasting impression on my life. I praise the Lord for all of them and thousands more like them around the world. They deserve recognition.

Almost from its inception the Church has realized the value of providing for its children a Christian education that is in harmony with biblical teachings. Adventist Christian education is based on the philosophy that God is the ultimate source of existence, wisdom, and truth. That we are created in His image as free moral agents. That although sin marred His perfect image in us, through Christ and His Holy Spirit, God is restoring fallen humanity to its original state. Therefore the purpose of Christian education, as stated by Ellen White, is:

> True education means more than the pursual of a certain course of study. It means more than a preparation for the life that now is. It has to do with the whole being, and with the whole period of existence possible to man. It is the harmonious development of the physical, the mental, and the spiritual powers. It prepares the student for the joy of service in this world and for the higher joy of wider service in the world to come.[98]

There are three eternal truths that every Christian child should learn early on to be able to understand who he is, where he came from, and what his destiny is.

1. God reigns.

   "The Lord God omnipotent reigneth" (Rev. 19:6) is the first and foremost truth. He is the Sovereign God—omnipotent, omniscient, and omnipresent—that is in control of the universe and everything in it, including Planet Earth. Nothing takes place without His notice. The capacity to think, every heartbeat, every breath you take originates with God.

2. God cares for and loves us.

   We were made in the image of God and His likeness (Gen. 1:26). He is our Maker and Sustainer. He loves us with an everlasting love (Jer. 31:3). We are precious in His sight. This truth will assure students that the Almighty God of heaven is deeply interested in them and loves them.

3. God has a plan for your life.

   God has a definite plan and purpose for each person in this world. This truth gives meaning, purpose, and direction to life. God has endowed each one of us with certain abilities, talents, and gifts which He desires us to develop to their fullest potential to His honor and glory. In doing this, we are not to depend on our own understanding, but "In all thy ways acknowledge Him and He shall direct thy paths" (Prov. 3:5, 6). "Before men can be truly wise, they must realize their dependence upon God, and be filled with His wisdom. God is the source of intellectual as well as spiritual power."[99]

We are to depend on Him as the apostle Paul states "I can do all things through him who strengthens me" (Phil. 4:13). By combining the intellectual with the spiritual, young men and women can reach the highest standard of God's ideal for them.

No life can be complete, satisfying, or rewarding if these three supreme truths are missing from our curriculum of education.

5

New Age Put to Music

Music is the international language. And if the enemy of our souls is seeking to sweep the world with his deceptive message, he cannot overlook the powerful influence of music. He is a master musician and composer, having been in charge of all the heavenly music before his fall. In the last three decades, the New Age movement has spread to all the world, largely in part through the media of music.

The Beatles—heralds of the New Age

Perhaps the most famous and influential popular music group of the '60s was the Beatles from Liverpool, England. The group (Ringo Starr on drums, Paul McCartney, John Lennon, and George Harrison on electric guitars) was greatly influenced by American rock 'n' roll and rhythm and blues. At the beginning of their career, the Beatles' style of music was like much of the music of the '50s, songs included, "I Want To Hold Your Hand," "Do You Want to Know a Secret?" and "Please Please Me." Later they sang more folk-like songs such as "Yesterday," "Michelle, " "And I Love Her."

But by 1967, the Beatles were into drugs. The next year John was charged with possession of drugs and fined, and George and his wife were arraigned on marijuana charges.[100] Not only were they using drugs, but some of their songs, like "Lucy in the Sky with

Diamonds" (LSD) from the album *Sgt. Pepper's Lonely Hearts Club Band* condoned drugs.

From drugs to Hinduism

From drugs they turned to Hinduism. George Harrison and his wife Pattie were the first to take an interest in Hinduism and its music. That prompted them in 1966 to go to India where George studied sitar (a lute-like instrument) under Ravi Shankar. While there, they were introduced to Shankar's guru. They also made a trip to Varanasi, old Benares, on the Ganges River, one of the most holy cities in India, where they attended a three-day religious festival. What they saw and what they heard in Varanasi, left a deep spiritual impression on them. After returning to England, they began studying the Indian religion. And in February of 1967, Pattie joined the Spiritual Regeneration movement where she learned transcendental meditation. In the meantime, George was devouring books on Hinduism and sharing his knowledge with the other members of the group.

In mid-August of 1967, the Maharishi Mahesh Yogi went to London to give public lectures on Transcendental Meditation (TM). The Beatles were introduced to him and to Transcendental Meditation, which had a tremendous influence on their lives. One of the concrete effects was that they dropped the use of drugs, with meditation taking its place. John reflected, "If we'd met Maharishi before we had taken LSD, we wouldn't have needed to take it."[101] Paul later said, "At the moment, I am finding what I am searching for by meditation, I hope I will get more out of meditation, so that I will have no need for drugs. . ." And Ringo had more of an evangelistic concern when he said, "I hope the fans will take up meditation instead of drugs."[102] This "spiritual awakening," as they considered it, became evident in their music and the Beatles became the first "singing evangelists" of New Age Hindu beliefs put to music.

George Harrison and Hare Krishna

In the 1970 Beatles album *All Things Must Pass*, George Harrison introduced a song dedicated to Hare Krishna entitled "My Sweet

Lord." Many Christians thought that song was a Christian song referring to Jesus as his "Sweet Lord." However, George was later quoted in *Upbeat Magazine* as saying:

> The idea behind "My Sweet Lord" was to take the people by surprise being that it sounded like a "pop song." The important thing was not to offend them, so I put a "hallelujah" chorus, so that when they got to the "Hare Krishna" they would be tapping their feet with the rhythm and singing together "hallelujah." It was like a hook with false security. All of a sudden they will be singing "Hare Krishna," without realizing what was taking place."[103]

George seemed to be obsessed with Hare Krishna, believing that Krishna was God, that God has many names such as Allah, Buddha, Jehovah, Rama, but that all were Krishna. He desperately wanted to see God as his song stated and the only way to do that, he believed, was through Krishna Consciousness and meditation. By chanting a Hare Krishna mantra, as was done in the background during the chorus of his song "My Sweet Lord," (Hare Krishna, Hare Krishna, Krishna Krishna, Hare Hare, Hare Rama, Hare Rama, Rama Rama, Hare Hare), one inevitably would reach Krishna Consciousness.[104]

John Lennon's "Imagine"

In 1971 John Lennon introduced more New Age philosophy in the lyrics of his songs entitled "Instant Karma" (karma, the total actions of life that determine one's fate in the next life, according to Hindus) and "Imagine," a song about a New Age utopia. The song "Imagine," which is still popular today having been translated into several languages and used in commercials, talks about imagining that there's no heaven and no hell, no countries, no religion, and everyone living in peace. These are all part of the New Age philosophy that emphasizes a global community instead of the various countries and nationalities; no conventional or traditional religions as we know them and no concept of retribution (hell) and no heaven as taught in the Bible, only enlightenment. It really turns out to be a call for people to join the New Age movement. John sings, "You may say I'm a dreamer, but I'm not the only one. I hope someday you'll join us and the world will be as one."[105]

John was also into the occult, largely because of his wife Yoko Ono, who ordered her life by her psychics. She believed in it so much that she made sure that their son, Sean, was born on John's birthday, October 9 (by cesarean section), because her psychics had told her that if her son was born on his father's birthday, he would inherit his father's soul when his father died.[106]

More Hinduism by Harrison

In 1973 George Harrison, in his album *Living in the Material World*, introduced two more songs promoting New Age Hindu beliefs. The song "Give Me Love" contains a line that states "keep me from birth" which is a reference to the Hindu teaching of "nirvana" or the leaving of the reincarnation cycle, entering into a state of spiritual, universal bliss. He also introduces in this song the Hindu "Om" chant. In the song "Living in the Material World," Harrison refers to reincarnation by stating his recollections or memories of the "Spiritual Sky." The prayer in this song is directed to a pantheistic, impersonal god present in all things. The song ends with Harrison's acquired pagan concept of salvation: "the Lord Sri Krishna's grace, my salvation."[107]

Beatlemania

The Beatles' music and philosophies had a tremendous influence on millions of teeny boppers, college students, and young adults as well, influencing them in the use of illicit drugs and then into New Age beliefs (karma and reincarnation) and practices (Eastern mystical meditation). Dr. Timothy Leary, the controversial philosopher of the Woodstock Nation, described their enormous popularity as "almost religious," referring to them as "inspired psalmists," "four hip evangelists," "young messiahs," and "divine agents." Leary considered them as "another divine intervention" as Christ had been 2000 years before, "to loosen things up and restore the beauty and laughter and harmony of the natural order."[108]

Abbey Hoffman, a militant hippie of the late 1960s, said of the Beatles, "The effect of something like *Sgt. Pepper's Lonely Hearts Club Band* on me and other activists, organizers, and counterculture people around the world was one of incredible impact, like starting a fire in a fireworks factory."[109]

Other musical groups like The Rolling Stones and The Grateful Dead contributed to putting the occult philosophies of New Age to music. *Dupree's Diamond News* magazine, which is dedicated to maintaining the spirit of Jerry Garcia, the Grateful Dead's deceased leader, among the "deadheads" (followers of the Grateful Dead), says in their statement of purpose:

> It is our fundamental belief that the music of the Grateful Dead can serve as a potent catalyst for the creative and spiritual growth of those who beckon to its call, and we attempt to express this potential in as many ways as possible. We are also *dedicated* to using this Experience as an opportunity for personal and planetary healing as well as keeping the Deadhead family together.[110]

This statement also expresses concepts and goals of the New Age movement: nonbiblical "creative and spiritual growth" and "personal" healing (self-enlightenment, self-awareness) and "planetary healing" (hard-core ecology), all of which are concerns of the New Age.

Hair—New Age spiritual gospel of Aquarius

The theater musical *Hair* also had a tremendous impact on the minds of young people on both sides of the Atlantic. Caryl Matriciana, author of *Gods of the New Age* was one of those who was converted into the New Age, along with thousands of other young people in her generation, by the message of *Hair*. It was at the end of the turbulent '60s, when she was twenty years old, that she and her parents returned from India to their motherland, England.

Hair for her opened the doors to a new world of escape from reality through the use of psychedelic drugs and Hindu beliefs. It was what could be called one of the most powerful New Age evangelistic efforts. *Hair* suddenly gave young people new hope for the problems of society and the world as they sang "Let the sunshine in." Caryl was enticed to taste the fruits of another consciousness through drugs, which unlocked the doors of her mind. She was invited to "pull down the blinds" of her mind for total self-awareness. She states that the lyrics set her and the young people in the audience traveling into their bodies and into inner worlds.

> We were led through guided imagery, visualization, rhythmic music, and enthusiastic energy to merge with the universe. Through powerful suggestion, colors meshed and individuals joined together in one cosmic force—a force I eventually learned to call "God."

> Our souls could be released from our bodies as we astrally projected and joined this "God." Coming into his presence, we touched him! "Oh, my God," I hummed with the cast, "your skin is soft, I love your face." I wept quietly in ecstasy. In my euphoric state I was lulled by the musical through many scenes and ideas. And those that made the deepest impression on me were the ones that led through the paths of India.[111]

In the movie version of *Hair*, Berger, the hero, sang "I am reincarnated and so are we all!" In essence, what he was doing was recalling his mystical experiences of India—yoga, reincarnation, and drugs—encouraging us that this was a way to help us evolve and develop. Caryl was encouraged to join the anthem of *Hair*, which was "Aquarius." This contains New Age astrological ideas such as the position of the moon "in the seventh house" and Jupiter's alignment with Mars as signs that a new astrological age (the Age of Aquarius) is dawning.

The lyrics of the song promise that wonderful things, including harmony, understanding, and sympathy, will abound in this new era.[112]

Looking back, Caryl realized the impact that the musical message of *Hair* had on her thinking, reasoning, religious outlook, attitudes, and morality as well as on millions of others like her worldwide. She stated that *Hair* was the foundation that prepared young people and the world for the philosophies and beliefs that underlie

New Age thinking today, the most influential mindset.[113] Caryl was one of those fortunate young people who eventually got out of the New Age movement through the confrontation of Christ's claims on her life. She has since dedicated her life to exposing the spiritual dangers of the New Age movement.

Categories of New Age music

There are basically two broad categories of New Age music: (1) Pop music that promotes New Age philosophy through its lyrics and (2) "Yuppie muzak," or music designed to inspire mystical meditative states.

New Age through lyrics

Since the days of the Beatles, there have been popular artists singing pop songs that promote the philosophies and beliefs of the New Age. The Bee Gees' 1979 album *Spirits Having Flown* carries references of reincarnation. They were also fascinated with the occult with Maurice and Robin claiming to have psychic ESP powers.[114] Prince, whose themes deal with eroticism occasionally mixed with religion, in his song "Sexuality," from the album *Sign 'o the Times*, sings about a second coming, a "New-Age revolution" which will be an era when anything goes.[115]

Other popular singers that have introduced New Age concepts have been Whitney Houston with her song "The Greatest Love," Mariah Carey in "Hero" (both promote the New Age concept of self-love), Elton John sings the lead song of *The Lion King*, "The Circle of Life," (which has reference to the cyclical life cycle of reincarnation). Vanessa Williams sings "The Colors of the Wind" from the movie *Pocahontas* which blatantly promotes the pantheistic and animistic idea that "every rock and tree and creature has a life, has a spirit, has a name."[116]

Pantheism is the pagan belief that a universal energy or an impersonal essence of God permeates all things, animate and inanimate. Animism teaches that everything has a spirit that can communicate with the human spirit.

So the first type of New Age music is that which promotes through its lyrics, either blatantly or subtly, the philosophies and beliefs of the New Age movement.

Muzak

"Yuppie muzak," or music designed to get one into altered states of consciousness, mystical meditation, is the second kind of New Age music. It is by far the most prolific type. You can go to any popular music store and find racks and racks of mystical meditative music entitled "New Age."

This concept of New Age music came about as professional musicians and composers embraced the philosophies and beliefs of the New Age movement. They then began using their talents to serve the movement. Muzak is New Age music defined more by the intention of the artist than by the style and range. But it is also intended to be used "as background music for meditation or for achieving some sort of altered state of consciousness."[117] Therefore, it can be boring when listened to in an ordinary state of mind.

Musical elements missing in New Age meditative music

Music, in the Western world, generally has four elements: melody, harmony, rhythm, and tempo (beat). New Age meditative music usually has no beat, melody, or rhythm. It has no melody that you can hum or whistle after listening to it. This music has become so popular today that the prestigious Grammy Awards in 1987 added a New Age music category.

Basically, it is composed of harmonic sounds, sometimes accompanied by mystical, ambient sounds of outer space, giving the sensation of being surrounded by an eerie presence. Meditative music also occasionally employs the use of beat or tempo and mystical chanting. It sometimes utilizes sounds of nature like the sound of rain, the rustling of leaves in the wind, sounds of the ocean, a running stream, the singing of birds, and sounds of porpoises. It is too bad that Satan has taken some of the elements of God's creation to incorporate with his subtle New Age meditative music to make it seem innocent and harmless. But don't be misled, New Age music, can be used to inspire a trance state, and can be a first step on a slippery path to other dangerous forms of New Age mystical meditation or altered states of consciousness. The dangers of Eastern mystical meditation and the differences between it and biblical meditation are discussed more fully in chapter 11.

Popular New Age artists

Popular artsits who are composing New Age music include Vangelis, Serrie, *Shakti*, Kitaro, Yanni, and Stephen Halpern.

Halpern

Stephen Halpern, for instance, has produced "many albums that clearly integrate Eastern mystical practices with his music." His *Spectrum Suite* is designed to focus on each of the seven chakras (Hindu energy-centers in the body). In Halpern's own words, he says, "In my work, I seek to align myself with that force, and to uplift the life energies of the performer and listener in order to bring them into closer attunement with their own God-Self."[118] He further states regarding the inspiration of his compositions that "The music is coming to me but not from me. Much of the music is channeled from a higher dimensional awareness; call it the presence of guides or higher universal powers."[119]

Kitaro

Kitaro, who is a popular Japanese performer and composer, has sold millions of albums. His album entitled *The Light of the Spirit* expresses the New Age universal ideas about the universe, human existence, nature, and the cosmos. "Kitaro . . . calls himself a 'musician of the new culture.' He considers his music part of his spiritual path and sees his role as that of a cultural change agent, helping others gain a fresh outlook on the world."[120]

Yanni

Yanni Chrysomallis and his live-in girlfriend, Linda Evans, are both involved in Eastern meditation. Linda is a follower of the famous trance channeler J. Z. Knight, who channels a spirit that identifies itself as a 3500-year-old warrior named Ramtha from the lost continent of Atlantis.[121] The front page of the *Los Angeles Times* business section, July 4, 1995, listed the top ten New Age albums as of July 3: #1 – Yanni's *Live at the Acropolis*; album #2 *Live at Red Rocks* by John Tesh; #3 *Shepherd Moons* by Enya; and #4 *In My Time* by Yanni.[122]

The cover of Yanni's album titled *Keys to Imagination* depicts a twilight scene of the earth and celestial bodies all encased in egg shells. Perhaps the symbolism is designed to convey the message that we are about to be born into a New Age.

Shakti

Shakti is a New Age musical group that features John McLaughlin on the guitar. McLaughlin's interest in New Age ideas began with study of Eastern philosophy and religion, and this led him to become a member of the English Theosophical Society in the 1960s. In the early '70s he became a follower of the guru Sri Chinmoy under whose suggestion McLaughlin changed his name, adding the prefix of "Mahavishnu," which means divine compassion, power and justice.[123]

Enigma

Perhaps one of the most demonic New Age mystical meditation albums is *Enigma.* The titles of the songs alone will alert any Christian that this is not an album that they want to listen to. Some of the titles are: "The Voice of Enigma," "Principles of Lust," "Mea Culpa," "The Voice and the Snake," "Knocking on Forbidden Doors." The lead number, which is titled "Voice of Enigma," includes vocal instructions. It is done through the voice of a woman mysteriously inviting the listener: "Good evening. This is the voice of Enigma." The voice then goes on to state that listeners are about to be taken to another world and suggests turning off the light, relaxing, and moving with the music.[124]

New Age music entry point into New Age

New Age music may seem to be innocent or amoral. But it can

be spiritually dangerous if it becomes an entry point into the New Age mindset that includes occult and pagan beliefs.

The Bible principle that we should apply in listening to music is recorded in Philippians 4:8

"Finally, brothers, whatever is true, whatever is noble, whatever is right, whatever is pure, whatever is lovely, whatever is admirable—if anything is excellent or praiseworthy—think about such things."

Perhaps the two words that summarize this whole passage are "right" and "pure." God does not want us to expose ourselves to pagan and occult influences that are contrary to His express will of holiness and separation from the unclean.

6

"Wolves in Sheep's Clothing"

The warning Jesus gave regarding "wolves in sheep's clothing" (Matt. 7:15) is apropos for this chapter. Shortly after my first New Age book, *The Danger Within*, was printed, I remember walking into one of our Adventist Book Centers to purchase some books for our friends. As I passed the cashier's counter, one of the ladies on duty recognized me and called out in a hateful tone of voice, "Elder Vasquez, why did you condemn M. Scott Peck in your book?" Slightly taken aback at this unprovoked attack, I replied, "Because he's a New Ager. Read his book again with this in mind and you will find that everything I said about him is true."

That incident took place in the middle of summer. At Christmas time I returned to the ABC to buy some more books for friends. Passing the cashier's counter again, I was stopped by the same cashier. Coming out from behind the counter to meet me, she addressed me again, this time with a slight grin. "You were right," she said. Apparently she had reread the book, and this time with a more critical eye was able to see the subtle (and sometimes not so subtle) entries of New Age thinking. The reason, I discovered, that she had been so upset with me the last time she saw me was because the previous Christmas she had purchased seven copies of M. Scott Peck's *The Road Less Traveled* and had given them out to her children and relatives. And then after she read my book, she realized that not only had she invested money in propagating New Age thinking, but she had the unpleasant task of informing her children and relatives of her naivete concerning this book.

It's not always easy to spot Christian writers who have incorporated New Age concepts into their writings, but believe me they are out there. Some of the better known ones are M. Scott Peck, Richard Foster, Laurie Beth Jones, and Matthew Fox. In pointing this out, I don't mean to condemn everything these writers have written. But we need to look at what they have to say with our eyes wide open, realizing that they do incorporate some New Age ideas in their material.

Morgan Scott Peck

Psychiatrist M. Scott Peck is probably the most widely known "Christian" New Age writer of the late '80s and '90s. His book *The Road Less Traveled*, published in 1978, was on the New York Times Best Seller list for a record 600-plus weeks. At last count it had sold over five million copies.[125]

But what a lot of people don't realize is that when Dr. Peck wrote *The Road Less Traveled*, he wasn't even a Christian. "I became a Christian," Peck stated,

> several years after *The Road Less Traveled* was published—and remember, the very first sentence in that book is the great Buddhist truth 'Life is difficult'. . .An important man said to me, 'Scotty, it was so clever of you the way you disguised your Christianity in *The Road Less Traveled* in order to get the Christian message across to people.' And I replied honestly, 'Well, I didn't disguise my Christianity. I wasn't a Christian.' [126]

M. Scott Peck, while studying world religions at the Friends Seminary, encountered and embraced Zen Buddhism and for twenty years dabbled with Zen.[127] He confessed that he didn't believe he could have become a Christian without having gone through Zen Buddhism.[128]

When He appeared on the Oprah Winfrey show on December 8, 1993, Oprah reiterated the high praise lavished on Dr. Peck all around the country when she said "Few writers have touched more lives than Dr. Peck, and few messages have empowered more people."[129]

Thus countless unsuspecting Christians have been deceived by the writings of M. Scott Peck because he couches Eastern mysticism and New Age thinking in Christian terms. Even though he doesn't claim to be an Eastern mystic or New Ager himself, when you read his books, it is very evident that he has not only embraced those philosophies but incorporated them in his spiritual pathway (beliefs). For instance, he says we need to "pay closer heed than we usually do in the West to the concept of reincarnation."[130] That "Christ and Buddha are not two different men, but one and the same."[131] That "God wants us to become Himself (or Herself or Itself). We are growing toward godhood. God is the goal of evolution."[132] That the essence of the original sin was that at the temptation, Adam and Eve failed to set up a "debate between the serpent and God,"[133] which is a symbolic dialog between good and evil. That "if you want to know the closest place to look for grace, it is within yourself. If you desire wisdom greater than your own, you can find it inside you" and that "our unconscious is God."[134]

Also in this book, Dr. Peck quotes extensively from Carl G. Jung (occult psychologist who had a spirit guide called "Philemon the Demon") and other authors like Joseph Campbell (mythologist) and Carlos Casteneda (anthropologist and apprentice of a Yaqui Indian sorcerer), all of whom have greatly influenced the New Age movement.

Some of Dr. Peck's other best-selling books are *People of the Lie* (1983) exploring the human psyche in an attempt to bring healing to the human evil in society; *The Different Drum,* a spiritual journey toward self-acceptance (1987); *A Bed By the Window* (1990), a novel exploring spiritual themes; and *Further Along The Road Less Traveled* (1993); the sequel to *The Road Less Traveled,* in which he continues the theme of forming your own spiritual pathway. All of the above listed works are tainted with New Age/New Spirituality thinking.

In his book, *The Different Drum, Community Making and Peace,* Peck teaches that the salvation of this world is through community and rules that he outlines in the book. "In and through community lies the salvation of the world." "I need you, and you me, for salvation."[135] On page 21 Peck states:

> Community neither comes naturally nor is it purchased cheaply. Demanding rules must both be learned and followed. But there are rules! Quite clear ones. Saving ones. They are not obscure. The purpose of this book is to teach these rules and encourage you to follow them. The hope of the book is that we will learn them first in our personal lives, then apply them universally. For that is how the world will be saved.[136]

By contrast, we believe that the individuals of this world can only be saved through the grace of Jesus Christ who gave His life on Calvary, not by community or manmade rules. And if Peck is not referring to salvation from sin and eternal death but to the preservation of this world, well, he's wrong there also. Because the Scriptures teach that God will finally destroy this world, purifying it with fire and then make all things new (Malachi 4:1; 2 Peter 3:7, 10, 13; Rev. 21:5).

On page 192 of *The Different Drum*, Peck teaches that we are connected to all things (humans and inanimate things), "a fitting together according to an ordinarily invisible fabric underlying the cosmos," which is a pantheistic/monistic worldview. These are just a few of the many examples that can be taken from this and other books written by M. Scott Peck. If you are going to read M. Scott Peck for your own spiritual edification, just remember that he's not a theologian. On the contrary, he's a New Age psychiatrist, and his beliefs permeate all his writings.

Richard Foster

Dr. Richard J. Foster is another popular Christian writer who has embraced some elements of neo-occult mysticism relating to the use of the imagination and meditation. Both of these occult mystical methods are frequently utilized by New Agers to communicate with their "spirit guides" and undergo out-of-the-body experiences.

Foster comes from the Society of Friends (Quaker) religious discipline that was established by George Fox. One of their principle tenets is that faith is based only on firsthand knowledge of Christ and not on anything else; not logic, reasoning, historical accounts, or even the Holy Scriptures. In other words, Quakers need not consult a preacher or even their Bibles to receive knowledge of the Holy Spirit—the so-called "inner light of Christ," because the "inner light" is present in every human heart.[137] To the Quakers, the "inner light" is at the same level as, and can supercede" the Scriptures.

Apparently Foster was greatly influenced by mystics such as Francis of Assissi, Ignatius of Loyola, Morton T. Kelsey, Carl Jung, and Evelyn Underhill since the jacket of *Celebration of Discipline* says that his book features the "best" of their ideas. Underhill, for one, was fascinated with mysticism and wrote several books on the subject: *The Mystic Way* in 1913; *Practical Mysticism* (1915) and *The Essentials of Mysticism* (1920).

Ignatius of Loyola was the founder of the Jesuit order who led a fierce persecution against Christians who wouldn't submit to Roman church authority; Morton Kelsey is an Episcopal priest and Jungian analyst who supports various occult practices and likened Jesus and His disciples to "shamans." These men apparently have helped form some of Foster's spiritual formation concepts.[138]

In Foster's suggested books for further study, Morton T. Kelsey's *The Other Side of Silence* is recommended as "the most important single book on the theology and psychology behind the experience of Christian meditation."[139] Morton Kelsey draws heavily from Carl Jung and Robert Assagioli. Assagioli's mother was the first Italian Theosophist. He was greatly influenced by Eastern philosophy and religion, studying mysticism (Hindu, Buddhist, and Christian). He founded psychosynthesis, a humanistic/transpersonal psychology, "perhaps the most mystical of modern psychologies."[140] Assagioli was also a "prominent student of New Age medium Alice Bailey."[141] Yet Foster has not only felt free to draw from this polluted source for himself but to recommend it to his readers.

Questionable elements in Foster's "Disciplines"

In Richard Foster's 1978 edition of *Celebration of Discipline: The Path to Spiritual Growth* (for which he received a "Writer of the Year" award), he recommended employing the "lotus position" of the Eastern religions for meditation. "The lotus position of Eastern religion is simply another example—not a law—of posture. . . . Place the hands on the knees, palms up in a gesture of receptivity."[142]

The "lotus position" is the most widely employed mystical meditation position used by the Hindus and Buddhists in which the meditator sits cross-legged, back erect, cupped hands on the knees, with thumb and forefinger touching, and eyes closed. This is not just a position of comfort or style for Eastern mystics. There is a definite mystical reason for choosing to meditate in this position.

Hindus, especially, believe that this is the best position to allow the free-flow of mystical energy in the body. This sitting position enhances the awakening of the sleeping coiled, snakelike "kundalini" at the "base chakra" that through meditation will rise all the way up to the "crown chakra" enabling one to achieve oneness with the universe or the One, or self-awareness with your divine self. The cupped hands act as "receptacles," somewhat like a satellite dish, to receive universal entity communication. When Christians adopt this yoga position for biblical meditation, they are adapting a pagan position of spiritual self-discipline and taking a major step toward the mystical metaphysical world of spiritualism.

When Dr. Foster describes his "fourth" form of meditation, he states that its objective is "to bring you into a deep inner communion with the Father where you look at Him and He looks at you."

The Bible does not encourage us to attempt to see God. That is part of the reward for the redeemed, not for man in his sinful state. The apostle John, in describing the Holy City, comments, "But the throne of God and of the Lamb shall be in it; and his servants shall serve Him and *they shall see His face*" (Rev. 22:3, 4). Although there are a very few recorded instances in the Bible of individuals seeing God (Moses and Jacob), our understanding from a biblical standpoint is that generally we, as sinful human beings, cannot see God and live (Exodus 33:20).

Foster also encourages his readers to use their fives senses, just as Ignatius of Loyola did, to experience the presence of God the Father or Christ the Son.

"Hence," Foster says, "you can actually encounter the living Christ in the event, be addressed by His voice and be touched by His healing power. It can be more than an exercise of the imagination; it can be a genuine confrontation. Jesus Christ will actually come to you."[143]

John Ankerberg and John Weldon, authors of the *Encyclopedia of New Age Beliefs*, caution that:

> Richard Foster discussed the use of the imagination to relive biblical events, which is fine up to a point. Unfortunately, the process is extended, and when he encourages contacting an "inner Jesus," no warnings of potential spiritism are given. The fact is that people have entered into spiritism as the result of contacting a spirit guide who claims to be Jesus.[144]

One need not go far to find examples of this kind of spiritual deception within "Christianity." Will Baron, who was a member of a "Christian" New Age church, in his book *Deceived by the New Age,* describes this very experience in which he came in contact with what he thought was "Christ."[145] This spirit turned out to be Satan.

A young Adventist lady who we will call Summer, after reading Will Baron's book, wrote to him stating:

> I too have gone through a deception, but it was unfortunately through "Christianity," and not the New Age. . . I had an eight year walk with God. . . "praying through the sanctuary" and listening to "God's voice" in prayer. I was heavily into impressions and signs. . . I went through complete hell for about a year and a half. When I emerged from the experience I was a shambles, dangerously depressed, very suicidal, with nothing going for me. I have survived this (current) year through the prayers of a few. . . . Despite the progress I've made this year, I'm still plagued by voices, dreams, mental images, and suicidal thoughts and desires. . . . I've distanced myself quite a bit from Christianity. I'm

bitter and have lots of blocks inside towards God.[146]

Foster's "Heavenly Ascent"

Part of Foster's fourth meditation involves a "heavenly ascent," better known to New Agers as "astral projection" or "out-of-body experiences"(OBE).

> After awhile there is a deep yearning within to go into the upper regions beyond the clouds. In your imagination allow your spiritual body, shining with light to rise out of your physical body. Look back so that you can see yourself lying in the grass and reassure your body that you will return momentarily. Imagine your spiritual self, alive and vibrant, rising up through the clouds and into the stratosphere. Observe your physical body, the knoll, and the forest shrink as you leave the earth. Go deeper and deeper into outer space until there is nothing except the warm presence of the eternal Creator. Rest in His presence. Listen quietly, anticipating the unanticipated. Note carefully any instruction given.[147]

When the Evangelicals read this, they flagged it. And even though Dr. Foster removed it from his revised 1978 and 1988 editions, it doesn't mean that he stopped believing in astral projections or "heavenly ascents" meditation experiences. Christian Research Institute International, an organization dedicated to dispelling error and the subtleties of New Age philosophy and practice which are creeping into the Christian faith, states:

> Mr. Foster is a Christian and much of what he says in the book is very helpful. However, he does appear to lack discernment between authentic and counterfeit spirituality. Many of the authorities he cites as experts on the devotional life were pantheists . . . Others were liberal or borderline occultic. . . . If a mature Christian wants to read the revised edition of *Celebration of Discipline* with the awareness of the above-mentioned difficulties, he can do so at his own discretion.[148]

Foster has no doubt contributed a "lot of good information" on spiritual formation. But when one reads his books, it should be with a critical eye because some of the things he teaches are from Eastern mystics and Western occultists. Even though there is solid Christian ground in Foster's books, there is also "quicksand" that can swallow up undiscerning Christians, casting them into the traps of the dark underground caverns of subtle Eastern mysticism.

Shirley MacLaine

Shirley MacLaine, the most celebrated New Ager of the '80s and '90s describes her first astral projection in her book *Out on a Limb*.

> I felt myself flow into the space, fill it, and float off, rising out of my body until I began to soar. I was aware that my body remained in the water. I looked down and saw it. David stood next to it. My spirit or mind or soul, or whatever it was, climbed higher into space. Right through the ceiling of the pool house and upward over the twilight river. I literally felt I was flying . . . wafting higher and higher until I could see the mountains and the landscape below me and I recognized what I had seen during the day.[149]

Shirley didn't really understand what had happened to her, but her friend and spiritual mentor David told her that her soul had left her body. "You mean I was astrally projecting just then?" Shirley asked.

"Sure," he said. "I was doing that this morning right here while you were off walking. I take trips all over the place . . . In the astral world you can go anywhere you feel like, meet all kinds of other souls too."[150]

Barney and astral projection

Even children are being introduced to the occult mystical concept of astral projection through children's TV programs such as *Barney and Friends*.

In a children's book entitled *Just Imagine*, Barney teaches astral projection to young children, in a very innocent and subtle way of course. The book features a child named Lori talking to her little stuffed animal—a purple Barney dinosaur—sharing her fears about moving to another town. Evidently her parents had just told her that they were moving. All of a sudden Barney becomes alive—bigger than life—as he says "You loved me so much that your love made me real!"[151] Then Barney soars into the sky and invites Lori to do the same. He tells her to use her imagination. "Lori closed her eyes tight and imagined that she could fly, too. Then Barney said the magic words: "SHIMBAREE, SHIMBARAH, SIMBAREE, SHIMBARAH!"[152]

So together they fly to Oakdale where she will be moving and Barney shows her the new house and her new school. Then he brings her spirit back to her body on the porch where he returns to his original form as a little stuffed dinosaur. This is a very elementary way of introducing astral projection or out of body experiences to children.

Difference between visions and OBEs

At this point you may be wondering, "What is so wrong with astral projections anyway? Didn't the apostle Paul and Ellen White both have out of body experiences?" Not quite! There is a big difference between the mystical OBEs and the visions that the apostle Paul and Ellen White had. Most astral projections or OBEs are self-induced through various altered states or trance states of consciousness achieved through mystical meditation or self-hypnosis.

Shirley MacLaine induced her OBE by breathing deeply and staring at a flickering candle until she felt that she became the flame itself. "I had no arms, no legs, no body, no physical form. I became the space in my mind. I felt myself flow into the space, fill it, and floated off, rising out of my body until I began to soar."[153] MacLaine used a lit candle. Other so-called "astral gateways" to aid New Age occultists into an astral plane or travel are symbols, images, and mandalas . Eastern mysticism teaches that besides our physical bodies we have an astral, ethereal, invisible, or ghostlike body that can separate itself from the physical body during an unconscious or altered state of consciousness. It also teaches that this ethereal soul is attached to the physical body by a thin silver umbilical-like cord, and when that cord snaps, death occurs.[154]

The vast majority of these mystical astral journeys are self-induced, whereas in the apostle Paul's case, recorded in 2 Cor. 12:1-7, he states that what he experienced was "a vision or a revelation" given to him by God. When the servants of God experienced "visions," they were always initiated by God. In the case of Ellen White, it was the same thing. All her visions were initiated by God, whether they occurred during her seasons of prayer or when she was speaking. She never desired visions for herself. In fact, she said that

> If I could have my choice and please God as well, I would rather die than have a vision, for every vision places me under great responsibility to bear testimonies of reproof and of warning, which has ever been against my feelings, causing me affliction of soul that is inexpressible. Never have I coveted my position, and yet I dare not resist the Spirit of God and seek an easier position.[155]

Astral projections or OBEs are common to the Hindu Yogis and Chinese. Shamans from tribal cultures claim that, "they can project themselves out of the body at will by achieving an ecstatic state of consciousness."[156] When a person is in a self-induced, altered state of consciousness, whether it be for mystical meditation or OBE, he is not in control of his mental faculties and is in danger of demonic influence and possession. On the other hand, when God's servants, such as the apostle Paul, John the Revelator or Ellen White received a vision or revelation, God was there to protect them.

Satan and his fallen angels know that there is a genuine unconscious state in which God initiates visions and revelations to His servants. For centuries they have tried to counterfeit this method of divine communication. Then how do we know which is which? The Bible clearly gives us some principles to test these supernatural manifestations:

1. "To the law and to the testimony: if they speak not according to this word, it is because there is no light in them" (Isa. 8:20).

2. The Bible states clearly the enmity between Satan and Christ (Gen. 3:15, 2 Cor. 6:14-17). God does not work with those that are involved with any forms of pagan or occult practices.

3. God always initiates the divine encounters. The occult encounters are often initiated by the subject or by demonic influence.

4. Since God initiates His encounters with His servants at His will, the men and women of God do not have to acquire special physical preparations or have someone else assist them. On the other hand, the occult mystics employ numerous techniques such as rhythmic breathing, meditative sitting positions, centering, guided imagery, reciting mantras, and focusing on images or mandalas.

Laurie Beth Jones

Laurie Beth Jones is a popular lecturer on leadership development who has written several books on the subject, including *Jesus CEO, Using Ancient Wisdom for Visionary Leadership*. Jones draws many good CEO principles from the life of Christ and from other biblical characters. However, upon close examination, you will find that her writings are sprinkled with New Age thinking.

On page 179, Jones states:

> History is full of stories of people who gave their lives for a cause that was noble and holy in their eyes. Perhaps it is because deep down, we know that we are made of stardust, not just dust, and are willing to give up what we have on earth in order to approach the heavens from whence we came.

Does she mean by this that we were reincarnated? She reveals the same sort of thinking about our pre-existence in heaven in her book *The Path* when she states: "We forget at birth, perhaps, who we were in heaven—and the gifts we had there. Sometimes the memory of who we 'were' in heaven before we 'are' on earth lingers through childhood."[157]

Here again is a concept that is a part of New Age thinking—that humans have forgotten that they are "divine," that they are gods. That's why there is an overwhelming concern to go "within" to discover their higher self, or God-self.

On page 295 under the title of "Affirmations for Leaders," Jones wrote: "I proudly say I AM, knowing clearly my strengths and God-given talents. I repeat my strengths to myself often, knowing my words are my wardrobe." All of us know that "I AM" is one of God's names.

When Moses asked God for a name to tell the Hebrews who sent him, God said: "I AM that I AM. Thus shalt thou say unto the children of Israel, I AM hath sent me unto you" (Exod. 3:14). Jesus also said "Verily, verily, I say unto you. Before Abraham was, I AM" (John 8:58).

This is a name of deity, and humans should never take that name as their own, affirming themselves by it. This is a belief of those in the New Age, or as some call it, the New Spirituality movement. They believe that they possess a god self. That they are divine. Therefore, they have no problem appropriating the ultimate name of God Himself to themselves for affirmation. This is plain and simple blasphemy.

On page 13 of *Jesus CEO*, Jones says Jesus declared that His mission was "to teach people about a better way of life" and that "He saw himself as a teacher and a healer."[158] Even though a major part of Jesus' ministry was devoted to teaching and healing, this was not His main mission. His mission was to be the *divine Saviour* of the world, for He came "to save that which was lost" (Matt 18:11). "Jesus," the name God told Mary to call Him, means Saviour "because he will save his people from their sins" (Matt. 1:21). New Agers don't feel that they need a Saviour. Therefore they don't accept Jesus as a Saviour, only as an enlightened Master or teacher, as Jones depicts Him. Teachers and healers don't necessarily have to be divine. But Christ was more than this. He was the Son of God. This may not appear to be a big issue, but it could be a subtle way of nullifying the unique mission of Jesus as Saviour.

On page 17, Jones states, "If only we believed in ourselves, the world would be a better place."[159] The New Age teaching is that the world will become a utopia of sorts when individual and global transformation takes place to usher in the Age of Aquarius, an age of peace, harmony, and prosperity. The Bible does not teach that the world will become better by believing in ourselves. On the contrary, the world will only be better when sin is totally eradicated and God will make all things new.

Laurie Beth Jones' leadership lecture

I attended a meeting one day where Laurie Beth Jones was giving a talk on leadership. There were several things she said that I had a question on, so after the meeting, I approached her and asked if I could ask her some questions. In her lecture she had said that we should affirm ourselves by saying "I AM" and that Jesus hung out with people at the taverns. When I asked her about the latter statement, she said, "I meant that metaphorically." Then she added, "He did drink wine with them." I commented, "We believe that He drank grape juice, unfermented grape juice." She replied, "Whatever."

I then asked her my second question. "You said that we should affirm ourselves by saying "I AM." Isn't that title only used for divinity—for God and Jesus?" She answered, "No."

Then I asked, "Where did you pick up on the 'four elements: water, fire, wind, and earth'?"

No sooner did I say this than she drew back in disgust. As she turned slightly around to her left she said, "This really makes me mad." Up to this time she had been totally immersed in our conversation, not realizing that there were about five or six people around us now intently listening to my questions and her answers. When she saw them, she quickly tried to regain her composure. Facing me again she apologetically said, "Oh I am not mad at you, but every time this comes up people think it's New Age, and it isn't."

"But," I added, "Don't the other non-Christian worldviews use the four elements a lot?"

"Yes they do, but that does not mean that they own them."

"I realize that," I told her. Recognizing how sensitive she was on this subject, I did not pursue it any further.

Wendy Kaminer, in a *Time* magazine article entitled "Why We Love Gurus," states that the New Age gurus of our day (such as Marianne Williamson, James Redfield, Matthew Fox) will expound on their particular fetish, but they give you no time to question their assertions. In fact,

> Most of these teachers are hostile to challenges. I have
> rarely seen an expert leave much time for questions after
> a talk. When audience participation is allowed, I've never
> heard anyone ask a probing critical question. When I've

respectfully argued with the experts or Goddess forbid,
corrected them, they have reacted with angry surprise.[160]

That was how my interaction with Ms. Jones seemed to me. Still, I ventured to ask her one last question. "You said in your lecture that you had a Methodist background and had accepted Jesus Christ."

She nodded "Yes." (However, she did not say she had accepted Him as her Saviour.)

"Do you belong to a Christian church somewhere in the country? I mean, are you a member in a local Christian church somewhere in the United States?"

She said, "No!"

I continued, "Then did you form your own spiritual pathway, gleaning from all the other world religions?"

"Yes," she answered.

I said, "Thank you. Those are all the questions I have."

I have discovered that this is true of other Christian writers who draw from the so-called "wisdom" of the Eastern mystical religious philosophies, adding it to their Christian base faith or religion.

The strait gate and narrow way

Christ tells us of a strait gate and narrow way that leads to life (Matt. 7:14). Few find this road. M. Scott Peck writes of a "road less traveled," which at first may sound like the same road. All counterfeits are hard to identify because they appear so much like the genuine. Peck's road runs parallel to the True Way for a while, but then passes through the land of Eastern religious philosophy which includes mystical meditation and reincarnation. And soon the "road less traveled" is no longer parallel to the True Way. It has subtly taken its travelers in another direction, 90 degrees from its original course.

If you look around, you'll see that "the road less traveled" is not what it was believed to be. Dr. Peck's "road" is a self-formed spiritual pathway, paved with nonbiblical Eastern religious philosophies. Some have been caught up in Foster's mystical "heavenly ascent." Others have gone down a spiritual pathway through the leadership principles drawn from the ancient wisdom, which includes not only the Holy Scriptures, but the nonbiblical worldview philosophies.

Wolves in sheepskins can be hard to spot and deceiving if we fail to look beneath the surface of their Christian veneered platitudes. The next time you pick up a book by one of these writers, or go to one of their seminars, write out some probing questions to help you understand where they're coming from and most importantly where they would like to take you.

7

Eco-Feminism, Pocahontas & The First Angel's Message

Eco-Feminism

What in the world, you may be wondering, do eco-feminism, *Pocahontas*, and an angel have in common? Well, believe it or not, there is a very definite tie between them.

Two of the most widely-discussed social issues of the '90s—the environmental, creation-care ("ecology") movement and the feminist movement—have captured and will continue to capture the attention of our society into the next millennium. While these are two enormously noble causes—one attempting to save the planet and the other to achieve equality for women—we will see, upon closer examination, that "hard-core" proponents of both are actually leading them astray.

For practical purposes, the environmental and feminist movements can each be divided into two camps—hard core and soft core. One of the major differences between the two groups is their philosophical view and understanding of reality; in other words, their worldview. Soft-core environmentalists are, by and large, Christians who embrace the theist (God-centered) worldview. On the other hand, the hard-core environmentalists have espoused non-biblical worldviews such as pantheism, Animism, Monism, Deism, Naturalism, or those containing elements of two or more worldviews.

A look at worldviews

Until recently, most of us have not concerned ourselves with worldviews. That was something we took for granted. People who were confronted with different worldviews were mainly missionaries who attempted to bring the gospel to peoples in nonChristian countries. However, because of the thousands of Asian immigrants who have come to America in the two last decades, and the increasing numbers of New Agers who embrace a different worldview, many Americans are coming in contact with people who have a different philosophy about how they view and understand reality.

Even though it may not seem to matter to some, the philosophy of how we understand and view the world we live in is of supreme importance, because it determines how we look at and relate to our world, God, and fellow humans. For example, some Hindus believe that they have millions of lives to live, so what is one life? They also believe that their lot in this life is a direct result of karma (the total of all their deeds done in their previous life). Therefore, there is very little pity or sympathy for a poor, maimed beggar because, according to this view, he is only paying for his past bad deeds (karma). And if something is done to relieve his situation, it will just mess up the necessary process. Another example is that some New Agers believe that they are gods and therefore seek to develop the god or goddess within. Since they are gods, they can do no wrong. Therefore, they don't need a Saviour. And since they are gods, they are immortal and don't really die. At death, they just enter another life cycle (reincarnation).

Theism is the belief in one omnipotent, omnipresent, and omniscient God, a personal, living God who created the earth and is Supreme Ruler and Sustainer of the universe. This biblical worldview, sometimes referred to as the Christian worldview, also includes belief in the Holy Trinity—God the Father, Jesus Christ the Son of God, and the Holy Spirit. Theism is the bedrock of Christian doctrines. Therefore, for the Christian, the theistic worldview is the basic doctrine that serves as a foundation for all the rest. It sets us miles apart, as far as the east is from the west, from the prevailing non-biblical pagan worldviews.

Pantheism, on the other hand, is the belief that God is in every element of the universe, that an essence of God or universal energy or force has permeated everything including Planet Earth. Pantheism plays a prominent role in the Hindu worldview.

Animism is the belief that all objects, animate or inanimate, including animals, plants, rocks, and other natural elements, have a soul and a spirit. Parts of these two worldviews, pantheism and animism, are shared by Hindus, Buddhists, and Native Americans.

Monism is the worldview which teaches that there is only one principle of being or ultimate substance, be it mind or matter. The theory is that reality is a unified whole. Buddhists sometimes liken the whole world and everything in it, including humans, to a massive orchestra, all playing their part to produce harmonious music. The most common phrase that expresses monism is "one is all and all is one." New Agers who embrace this philosophy strive for mystical oneness with the universe.

Deism is the belief in a Creator God who put the universe in motion, then left it alone to carry on. In this worldview, God is not involved with our day-to-day concerns, problems, or events, but only "watching from a distance" just like Bette Midler's song says. This was the belief that William Miller, the founder of the Millerite movement, held before he became a preacher of the Second Coming.

Naturalism is the theory that all phenomena are derived from natural causes and can be explained by logic or scientific laws without reference to a plan or purpose. This is an evolutionary theory that is held by many scientists and secular humanists. Naturalists only study nature, and since humans are a part of nature, a branch of Naturalism is Secular Humanism. Secular humanists, in turn, seek to develop the human potential within. This worldview supposedly frees a person from any claims God has on the human race.

There are other worldview theories, but they will not be mentioned here, mainly because they overlap or are similar to the ones mentioned above. Now with this brief background, let's get back to the subject.

The marriage of convenience

Hard-core environmentalists believe that the earth not only has life on it but is itself a living organism, or a living being, with a spirit called Mother Earth or goddess Gaia who is to be venerated and worshiped.[161] This is a pantheistic/animistic worldview which denies the existence of God as a personal, living Creator and Sustainer of our planet.

Hard-core feminists, who originally worked to gain "full inclusion of women in political rights and economic access to employment" have gone far beyond that objective. Because they believe that males have ravaged the land, abused and dominated women, they have become antagonistic toward the whole patriarchal system in our society. They reject anything that smacks of the biblical, patriarchal (male-domi-nated) system. Eco-feminism can be defined as: the union of the radical ecology movement, or what has been called 'deep ecology,' and femi-nism."[162] In the late eighties these two causes, environmentalism and feminism, joined ranks and called their union eco-feminism.

Hard-core environmental movement

When you fly into Los Angeles, the one noticeable "airmark" that first greets you is the smog. It hovers over the city like a dingy fog. But Los Angeles is not the only place where "air" can be seen. This is also true of other major metropolitan areas like Denver, Chi-cago, and Washington, D.C. Some days the smog levels in these cities are "unhealthful" (pollutants standard Index, or PSI, is be-tween 101-199) "very unhealthful," (PSI 200-300) and "hazardous" (PSI 301-500). The last rating indicates the need to restrict outdoor activities or stay indoors if possible.

Remember when everybody drank water from the tap? Today, that's not the norm. Bottled "pure" drinking water is a multi-million dollar business because much of the tap drinking water is either pol-luted or contains dangerous levels of minerals.

The increasingly toxic chemical waste dumping sites that are dot-ting our nation, the destruction of the rain forests, and senseless killing of porpoises and seals are all concerns of national and international proportions. Cities worldwide are trying to stem the ecological erosion with programs such as recycling, conservation, stiffer anti-pollution laws, and educating people about their environmental responsibilities. But even though these commendable measures are being taken, it is evident, when you see all the litter on our beaches, inner harbors, highways, and city streets, that we still have a long way to go in cleaning up our planet. Too many people just don't care.

Of all people, we Christians should be very concerned about the ecology, mainly because of our worldview philosophy or the way we look at and understand reality. In other words, a worldview philosophy is what gives meaning to what we see and experience in our world. As mentioned before, it is so important because it forms the basis for our philosophical, spiritual, and futuristic beliefs. These in turn determine our actions and lifestyles.

The Christian worldview is a creationist view that recognizes God as the Creator and Sustainer of the earth. Within this worldview or philosophy we understand that men and women were created differently from the rest of creation—that humans were made in the image of God, and therefore are superior to the rest of creation. We were made the custodians and stewards of God's creation. Thus, we should be "green," "creation-care" Christians. This awesome responsibility calls for each one of us to cultivate, enhance, protect, and preserve our environment as much as possible. The command "to subdue" the land and "have dominion" (Gen. 1:28) was never intended as a license for humans to exploit, ravish, pollute, or destroy the planet and its inhabitants.

Instead, we should be conservationists, participating in the recycling programs of our communities and keeping our automobiles in tune to help reduce air pollution. It would be commendable if our Pathfinders or youth groups (with proper supervision and permission) would volunteer to clean up two or three miles of county or state highway or a beach site. Environmental concerns and participation of this kind would fall under the general category of creationist "soft-core" environmentalists.

Bio-centric equality

Hard-core environmentalists go a step or two beyond the creationist view. They believe in a concept called "bio-centric equality."

What this means is that if you were to take a plot of land, say two thousand acres, everything on that piece of land would have equal standing—the pine trees, the plants, the stream, the spotted owl, the deer, the wolves, the raccoons, the fireflies, and even the rancher and his family. All would have equal value. If one is threatening the existence of another, it would have to be eliminated in order to protect or maintain an ecological balance. This belief, carried to its logical conclusion, could allow so-called "subhuman" people groups to be eliminated in the name of maintaining ecological balance.

Bio-centric equality is espoused because many hard-core environmentalist have adopted a pantheistic/animist worldview. To them everything that is on the earth—plants, animals, and humans—has equal value because they all have the same universal energy, life-giving force, spirit, or self-sustaining essence of a god quality in them. Thus all have spirits that can connect with each other.

Like Hindus and Buddhists, hard-core pantheistic/animistic worldview environmentalists believe that all living things are sacred because the same god-like essence or universal energy ("prana" or "chi") that is in humans is in all the rest of creation as well. For this reason many have become vegetarians. They won't eat anything that has a face with eyes.

In India, for example, you won't see Hindus hammering nails into trees because they believe in the transmigration of life (reincarnation from one species to another) and the tree may contain the spirit of a loved one. For the same reason, many Hindus are vegetarians.

Some eco-feminists would have us believe that "pneuma," God's breath or spirit, is also God's soul which permeates even the very air that we breathe; and since all creation shares God's breath, all creation shares the very soul of God. This is just another way of describing pantheism.

Not all creation stands with equal value before the Creator. With the exception of Adam and Eve, when God made the earth and everything in it, He merely spoke them into being. He commanded and the elements obeyed His voice. "By the word of the Lord were the heavens made; and the host of them by the breath of His mouth" (Psalm 33:6). "For He spake, and it was done; He commanded, and it stood fast" (Psalm 33:9).

But when it came to making man, God did something special. He went down to the river's bed, got down on His knees, gathered some clay, and carefully formed a tall, perfectly symmetrical man. There was Adam, a perfect specimen of a man in every respect. There was only one thing missing—he was lifeless and inanimate. So God, the source life, drew close to him and blew into his nostrils the breath of life; and man became a living being (Genesis 2:7). Instantly all of Adam's vital organs began to function. His heart started pumping the blood to all the extremities of the body. The lungs filled with fresh air and inflated for the first time. It felt good. Then Adam opened his eyes and looked into the holy face of his Divine Creator for the very first time. I'm sure they took time to converse and get acquainted.

Then God made Eve from one of Adam's ribs. We are not told exactly how that was done, except that Adam was put to sleep for the operation. Nevertheless, Eve was also created, a perfect, beautiful companion for Adam. "So God created man in His own image, in the image of God created He him; male and female created He them" (Genesis 1:27). Nothing else was created in God's image except the human species. Nothing else was created with the personal attention and detailed care that was given to the creation of man and woman. After Creation was completed, God gave our first parents dominion over His creation to care for it (Gen. 1:28).

Four thousand years later when Jesus came to live among the sinful human race and then died on Calvary's cross, He didn't die to atone for the sins and the salvation of the Blue Spruce, the spotted owl, the deer, the raccoon, the streams, or fireflies. He died for you and me. We were made in the image of God, and that sets us on a completely different plane from the rest of creation. Thus as Christians, we cannot accept the hard-core philosophy of "bio-centric equality." That is pantheistic, animistic, and diametrically opposed to the biblical teachings.

Al Gore and ecology

United States Vice President Al Gore, at the very outset of his book *Earth in the Balance, Ecology and the Human Spirit* (written while he was a senator from Tennessee) states that the root cause for our global ecological crisis is that we have "lost our feeling of connectedness to the rest of nature."[163] However, the real problem for the ecological crisis we are in is not that we are out of touch with nature, but instead that we are out of touch with God Himself.

The Vice President further states that if we Christians were more open-minded to the religious teachings of the non-Christians, we would discover a richness of spiritual resource and wisdom that may prove, "important where our global civilization's responsibility for the earth is concerned."[164]

Gore's advice that Christians should look to the world's pagan religions for wisdom and spirituality to help solve the ecological problems should raise a definite red flag in any thinking Christian's mind.

Flagging the environmental movement

Many of the hard-core environmentalists have embraced non-biblical worldviews and attract to their ranks New Agers who share these beliefs. It is important to know what worldviews the environmental movement upholds in order to understand where they are headed as well as to avoid spiritual seduction.

Tony Campolo, a Christian author and much sought-after youth speaker, raised the following red flag on the popular environmental movements of the day.

> If we're serious about leading our society in a commitment to saving the environment, we will have to work with people outside the church and that means we will inevitably end up in dialogue with New Agers. They are everywhere. It is almost impossible these days to go to a conference dealing with ecological issues without meeting them. They wrote many of the books on the environment. And what they say and how they say it is often attractive enough to seduce the unprepared into a mind-

set estranged from biblical Christianity. This has happened time and time again. Some of the most prominent thinkers in the New Age movement started off as rather traditional Christians, seeking ways of thinking about nature that might raise the church's consciousness on environmental issues and concerns.

The increasing affinity the New Age movement has with the environmental movement has made many evangelical leaders suspicious of anyone who is involved in creation-care concerns. They have seen too many cases in which involvement with environmental issues was the first step into the strange, cultic world of New Age thinking. They are aware that, in some extreme cases, environmental concerns have led church members into the occult and even into Satanism.[165]

The caution given here is worth heeding. The environmental movements of the day are not all kosher. If we Christians unite with them or support them in any way, it could be viewed as condoning their nonbiblical worldviews, mainly pantheism. But worse yet is the spiritual danger that may come from working too closely with those whose worldview does not regard the divine Creator.

Pantheism once knocked at the door of the Adventist Church

Pantheism once knocked at the door of the Adventist Church, you may recall. It was in the person of Dr. John Harvey Kellogg. At a very early age, Kellogg had been taken into Ellen G. White's home. She helped him receive the best medical education possible in the late 1800s. Later, Kellogg as we know, became a very successful medical doctor and director of the world-renowned Battle Creek Sanitarium, the largest of its kind in the world. It became so famous that the world's monarchs, presidents, and men of wealth came from far and near to be treated there.

Success, however, if not tempered with humility, has a tendency to go to one's head, and this was the case with Dr. Kellogg. He came to believe that he was beyond reproach. At the height of his success, he began embracing pantheistic concepts, as opposed to the theistic position held by the Church. Then, when he was asked to write a book on health to raise funds for education, he ventured out, introducing the pantheistic belief in the essence of God in all of nature. In his book entitled *The Living Temple*, he wrote,

> So there is present in the tree a power which creates and maintains it, a tree-maker in the tree, a flower-maker in the flower—a divine architect who understands every law of proportion, an infinite artist who possesses a limitless power of expression in color and form; there is, in all the world about us, an infinite, divine, though invisible presence, to which the unenlightened may be blind, and which is ever declaring itself by its ceaseless, beneficent activity.[166]

When his book was reviewed by some of the church's theologians, they detected the false philosophy. For the next two years, Mrs. White and the brethren worked with Dr. Kellogg, but to no avail. He had departed from the biblical worldview, embraced a pantheistic worldview, and could not be dissuaded. There was nothing else left to do but disfellowship him from the Adventist Church. This has to be one of the saddest chapters in the history of the church. One of the brightest, visionary members—lost to the world. And the Battle Creek Sanitarium, being one of the most potent means of sharing the truth to the world, was lost along with him. What a loss to the cause of God.

The servant of the Lord later wrote, "Not one thread of pantheism is to be drawn into the web."[167] Pantheism does away with a personal God who is very much involved with the concerns and events that take place in the world. It does away with Jesus the Saviour of the world. It removes the claims that God has on each one of us. Therefore, not one trace of it should taint our thinking and understanding of the reality that surrounds us. Creation bears the evidence of God's creative power and glory, not of some impersonal, ethereal, universal energy.

Oppression of women around the world

If you look around this old world of ours, you will discover that there aren't too many places that are friendly to women. In Saudi Arabia, Iraq and Iran, for instance, women are not even permitted to drive. In Algeria more than 500 women have recently been killed by armed factions—some for just being known as feminists and others for merely showing their unveiled faces. In Poland women have no right to abortions. In Russia, with its post-Communist economic burst, an office secretarial job can include the requirement to sleep with the boss. In Brazil, wife murderers routinely get off with only a slap on the wrist. Or take India, where more than 6000 women a year are killed by their husbands and in-laws merely so that they can collect a second dowry on another wife. Ms. Benazir Bhutto, former prime minister of Pakistan, who won high praise for her presentation at the Beijing Women's Conference, never said anything about the female rape victims in her country who are subject to prison sentences for "adultery."

If we were to compare America with all of these other countries, it would appear that America is miles ahead in respect to women's rights. In some respects it is. Eighty years ago, women could not vote. Today they represent the largest single segment of the voting force in our country. Forty years ago, American women could not claim equal rights to employment, housing, education, or credit. Today their rights to these things and others are written in the law books of the land. There is no question that much progress has been made in America toward full and equal citizenship for women.

Feminists and Father God

Hard-core feminists, however, see the patriarchal system as sexist, and in an attempt to gain equality they are doing all they can to change our patriarchal society. The Bible is even labeled as "sexist." Patricia Aberdeen, wife of John Naisbitt and co-author of *Reinventing the Corporation* and *Megatrends 2000* says in her book *Megatrends for Women,* that "Central to women's spiritual quest is outright rejection of the notion that God is somehow male."[168] And to prove her point she quotes several women in ministry. One is Sister Mary Daly, associate professor of theology at Boston College, who says, "As long as God is a male, the male is God." Another is Dr. Barbara Thiering, theologian at the University of Sydney. She says that "God as male, as father, is only a metaphor but . . . the church has taken it literally."

However, the fact remains that Jesus was the only One who had ever seen God and knew Him personally and He referred to the Almighty as "My Father" and "Our Father." Many Christians worship God in the form of the Trinity: Father, Son, and Spirit. Sister Sandra Schneiders, another hard-core feminist sacrilegiously writes, "but in many people's imagination . . . this comes down to an old man, a young man, and a bird. First, God is not three people, much less three males." She argues that God is better described as "divine communicator, divine communication, and redeemer . . . divine energy, mover, transforming power."[169] This sounds like pantheism to me.

Patricia Aberdeen further states that, "Whether a woman espouses traditional religion, the New Age spirituality or atheism, her sense of personal power is enhanced by the mythology of the Goddess, which awakens confidence, belonging and self-esteem."[170]

When Cybil Shepard, received her Golden Globe award in Hollywood in January of 1996, she did so with these words of gratefulness: "I want to thank the great goddess in all her various forms . . ." This was a way of identifying herself with the popular radical feminist movement of the day.

By the way, in case you hadn't guessed it, both John and Patricia Naisbitt are committed New Agers. When *Newsweek* magazine did a lifestyle story on this couple, it stated that in "commendable New Age style they meditate together for 20 minutes each day." Also "both believe in reincarnation and think the reason they get along so well together is that they knew each other in a previous life."[171]

Profile of a feminist

You might be wondering who in the world really believes these things anyway? You don't know any one that does. Well they are out there, believe me. Thousands of them, perhaps millions. The sociological profile of the hard-core feminist is: "White, of middle-class origin, fairly well educated (beyond high school), of Jewish or Christian background (usually, though not always having had a significant amount of religious training), in their thirties or forties, and disproportionately lesbian. There are many women who are exceptions to one or more (or all) of these rules, but most approximate this profile."[172]

Disney gets involved

The motion picture industry has been known to promote many popular causes and this one is no exception. Walt Disney studios did so with *Pocahontas,* a full-length animated film, based on a real historical, Native American heroine.

If you haven't noticed, Disney, the hallmark of "wholesome" family-oriented entertainment of the fifties, has changed its colors. Few people realize that Disney subsidiaries like Miramax have distributed films like *Kids*—"a raw depiction of a sex-obsessed, drug-bleary day in the life of some New York City teens," and *Priest,* the controversial film about a gay and a sexually active straight priest, which came into scrutiny following former Senator Bob Dole's attack on Hollywood for contributing to the decline of the morality of the nation. As a protest, Dole's wife, Libby, quickly announced that she was selling her more than $15,000 worth of stock in Walt Disney, Inc.

A child's films with adult issues

Recent full-length animated films produced by Disney, such as *Aladdin, The Little Mermaid, Beauty and the Beast,* and *The Lion King,* have all introduced New Age beliefs and philosophies. Although Pocahontas has been marketed as a children's film, it carries some heavy adult issues. *Premiere Magazine* pointed out that *Pocahontas,* "gets into some meaty issues—the clash of cultures, prejudice, feminism, ecology, even colonialism. . . . It is definitely more of an adult movie than its predecessors."[173] *Time* magazine called this courageous and self-determined Pocahontas the first "eco-feminist," "the portrait of a princess of the spirit."[174]

While the viewers are being entertained with this epic of adventure and romance, the movie, through Pocahontas, ingeniously confronts them with the underlying agenda of clashing issues such as culture, ecology, worldviews and feminism. "Whose worldviews and feminist roles are superior?" is the important question the viewers are gently confronted with.

Pocahontas and animist/pantheistic worldview

In the movie, Pocahontas is portrayed as Chief Powhatan's beautiful, courageous, 20 year-old daughter who exhibits Native American pantheistic beliefs and the '90s feminist views. She has a dream in which an arrow is spinning around in front of her. Although she doesn't know the meaning of the dream, she knows someone who does—Grandmother Willow.

Grandmother Willow is the spirit of a 400-year-old willow tree deep in the forest. Grandmother Willow is Pocahontas' confidante spirit guide whom she often visits for counsel. One day she stops to see Grandmother Willow, accompanied by Meeko the raccoon, her constant companion. When she asks Grandmother Willow what her dream means, she is told that it seemed that this arrow was pointing Pocahontas down her path or destiny. "But what is my path?" Pocahontas asks. Grandmother Willow responds by telling her "Listen. All around you are spirits. They live in the earth, the water, the sky. If you listen, they will guide you."

This spiritualistic concept goes back to the earliest forms of nonbiblical worldviews of animism mixed with pantheism—a worldview that teaches that all of nature, trees, birds, animals, and all the elements like rain and wind, as well as humans, have a kindred spirit. It teaches that a supernatural universal energy or spirit permeates everything we see and sense. It teaches a way of understanding the reality of the world totally opposite to the biblical worldview of creationism.

Native Americans have traditionally viewed nature in varying forms of animism and pantheism. Animists believe that the elements, creatures and plant life all have spirits which can communicate with humans and even direct their destiny if they "listen," as Grandmother Willow put it, with their "heart"—their intuitive, perceptive, spiritualistic psyche. Animism teaches that we are a part of this mystical world filled with spirits—good and evil.

In the movie, Pocahontas represents (1) the animist/pantheistic worldview in which a supernatural essence permeates all of nature and humans; (2) the "primitive, heathen, uncultured, uneducated, savage people," (3) the environmental concerns of the ecology movements of our day; and (4) the feminist crusade of the '90s.

Captain John Smith's conversion

Captain John Smith, on the other hand, represents (1) the creationist, biblical view of the world; (2) the "cultured, educated, civilized" people; (3) the exploiters of the land and opportunists who have little or no regard for the land's ecology or its inhabitants, (4) the traditional, patriarchal, dominant role of males in society, which, by the way, Pocahontas' father shares.

One day, as the movie story line goes, Pocahontas and Smith meet. After their get-acquainted hide-and-seek game, they begin to discuss their differences. One time, Smith refers to her people as "savages," to which she responds, "Why, because we're not like you?" And before he realizes it, she takes him by the hand and runs through the forest with him as she teaches him how all nature—animals, plants, the wind, the clouds, even people are alive and animated by spirits that can connect with each other. She is so convincing and aggressive that Smith is convinced and before the day is over, he is a changed man. He experiences a paradigm shift, a new way of looking at and understanding the reality of his world. He not only exchanges his biblical creationist worldview for her animist/pantheistic worldview, but also experiences a spiritualist encounter (seance) when he talks with the spirit of the 400-year-old tree in the forest.

Smith is converted, or rather, "enlightened" and sees his people as the exploiters of the land, seeking for gold and riches while destroying the environment in their wake. Pocahontas' ways of co-existing and communicating with nature seem superior. No doubt he wondered, "Who has it right ? Us or them? Who are the real 'savages'?" One thing is for certain, the love bug had bitten them both and a tender but forbidden romance ensues, which adds to the already mounting tensions between the natives and the English settlers.

The cultural clash soon results in a declaration of war. The Native Americans determine to wipe out the newcomers while John Ratcliffe, the leader of the Jamestown expedition, is planning the same. Since the English have the superior "fire power" they decide to become the aggressors.

Chief Powhatan forbids anyone from his tribe to associate with the "white settlers." But Pocahontas, portraying a non-traditional, feminist role, ignores her father's command, even though he is the supreme patriarch, the law-giver and law-enforcer, the one everyone "must obey, not only as a king, but as a god"[175] of her people. She proves to be more courageous and daring than her father's warriors.

When the Native Americans capture Captain Smith and Chief Powhatan is about to kill him with a stone-head tomahawk, Pocahontas breaks from the watching crowd and runs over to where Smith is about to be executed and puts her head on his head to save his life. Her father is awestruck by her bravery and spares Smith's life. Pocahontas then convinces her father to coexist with the English settlers rather than fight them. In short this brings peace and harmony between the Powhatans and the settlers. Her father's famous words that day were, "My daughter speaks wisdom beyond her years."

The rest of the story

What is wrong with all of this? Aren't the English settlers the bad guys? Apparently. But, as Paul Harvey would say, "Let me tell you 'the rest of the story.'" The story and screenplay writers, Tom Sito, Carl Binder, Susannah Grant, and Philip LaZebnik have rewritten history for us, which is common these days in Hollywood. Although the movie *Pocahontas* is based on a real story, this time the names, places, and plots were not changed to protect the innocent, but instead, to greatly enhance, exaggerate, and showcase the "eco-feminist" agenda.

In the best historical account that we have of Princess Pocahontas, we find that she was one of the twenty-seven children that chief Powhatan had with his many wives, she being his favorite. She was only about 12 or 13 years old when she supposedly saved the life of Captain John Smith. According to William Strachey's book *The Histories of Travel into Virginia Britannia*, Pocahontas married a Native American chief from her own tribe when she was 14 years of age.

The following year she was lured aboard an English ship and forced to live as a white woman. There she met John Rolfe and married him. She quickly learned to speak English and took Bible studies. Later she was converted to the Christian faith and became a member of the Church of England. At her baptism she was given the Christian name of Rebecca. In 1616 she sailed to London, England, with her husband where she was well received by the queen of England. That same year she bore her husband a son whom they named Thomas. On a return trip to Jamestown, Virginia, the following year, she died of what some say was small pox. Others think it was tuberculosis. Her son, Thomas Rolfe, became a prominent figure in the development of Jamestown.[176]

In the movie, it is Pocahontas who takes Smith under her wing and teaches him the ways of animism/pantheism. But in the real-life episode, it was Pocahontas who was converted from heathenism to Christianity, from her animist/pantheistic worldview to a biblical theist/creationist worldview. It is also uncertain whether or not the account of saving Captain Smith's life actually happened. Captain Smith's first recordings of his experiences never mentioned this heroic incident. It's also hard to believe that a twelve- or thirteen-year-old could have stopped an execution of this nature, and then talked sense to her father convincing him not to fight the settlers. You may say, "Who cares if they didn't get it right?" The answer is, you should, because you should know what the eco-feminists are up to.

The first angel's message of Revelation 14:6, 7

The three angels' messages of Revelation 14 have always been part of the heart and sinew of the Advent message, and for good reason, for they represent the final warning messages to the people of the world before the second coming of Jesus.

The first angel's message (Rev. 14:6, 7) addresses not only worship on the Seventh-day Sabbath but also the true worldviews.

"And I saw another angel fly in the midst of heaven, having the everlasting gospel to preach unto them that dwell on the earth, and to every nation, and kindred, and tongue, and people, saying with a loud voice, Fear God, and give glory to him; for the hour of his judgment is come: and worship him that made heaven, and earth, and the sea, and the fountains of waters."

Verse 6 gives the scope of the message. This message is to go to the entire world, to all the inhabitants of planet Earth. Not one people group is to be left out. Jesus made reference to this when He said, "Other sheep I have, which are not of this fold: them also I must bring" (John 10: 16).

Verse 7 of Revelation 14 is a concise statement of God's message for His world in need of salvation. It is a wake-up call to the inhabitants of the world that we are living in the time of God's judgment of those who claim to have accepted Jesus Christ as their Saviour. It calls attention to the Sabbath, the true day of worship that points not only to Creation week but to the Creator. "In the beginning God created the heavens and the earth" (Gen. 1:1). But it does more than that. It also makes reference to theism, the only true worldview. There is no pantheism, animism, deism, monism, or naturalism. All these are counterfeits, inventions of the pagan people inspired by the enemy of our souls.

As we draw closer to the second coming of Christ, worldviews will play a more prominent role in the debate over the Sabbath and the rationale for keeping it holy. The environmental and feminist issues of today are important, but let us be careful that in supporting them we don't become "bedfellows" with environmentalists and feminists who promote the pantheistic and animistic spirit of Mother Earth (Gaia) and goddess movements of the New Age.

8

Angels—Friends or Foes?

The obsession with angels

All of a sudden it seems there has been a celestial invasion of angels. I mean all kinds of angels—invisible and visible, archangels, guardian angels, healing angels, female angels, little naked chubby baby angels, and even angels of death. The truth is that there are indeed heavenly beings that we call "angels," and the Bible is the first to substantiate this. But dispelling the mystery and confusion surrounding these beings is the burden of this chapter.

In the last decade or so, the proliferation of angel art, poetry, books, ceramic figurines, movies, TV programs, Broadway plays, boutiques, newsletters, and seminars has been overwhelming. Even higher centers of learning such as Harvard Divinity School and Boston College offer courses on angels.

Angel jewelry is so popular that even Hillary Rodham Clinton wears a pair of gold angel wings on days when she feels she needs help.[177] Marcia Clark, the leading prosecuting attorney at the O.J. Simpson murder trial, on occasion wore an angel pin, which, by the way, Johnny Cochran, the defense attorney, complained about to Judge Lance Ito.

The polls indicate that almost 70% of adult Americans, including the X-generation, believe in angels,[178] which translates into almost 200 million Americans. Half of the world's population, or an estimated three billion, accept the existence of angels.[179] *Time* magazine recognized this in its 1993 issue on angels and stated that: "If there is such a thing as a universal idea, common across cultures and through the centuries, the belief in angels comes close to it."[180]

This angel phenomenon has a lot of people asking questions about these supernatural, lightsome spirit beings, unbound by time, space, and human weakness. What exactly is their nature? What is their mission in heaven and here on earth? Why do they appear to some people and not to others? What does the Bible teach about angels? Are angels also mixed up with the New Age?

Angels and the movies

The recent angel craze has prompted Hollywood and the TV networks to produce angel movies to meet popular demand. *The Preacher's Wife*, with Denzel Washington and Whitney Houston, and *Michael*, starring John Travolta as the angel Michael, have contributed to the prevailing New Age concept of angels. Even the 1946 classic *It's a Wonderful Life* contributes to the belief in nonbiblical ideas about angels.

1. *It's a Wonderful Life*

In *It's a Wonderful Life*, Jimmy Stewart, struggling to do well in his small town feels he has failed and tries to take his life. His attempt is averted when Clarence, his "guardian angel", is sent to him from heaven. In their dialogue, George Bailey (Jimmy Stewart) says in desperation that he wished he had never been born. Clarence arranges to give him his wish, just to teach him a lesson. He then reveals to him what the town would be like without him and eventually convinces George that his life touched and positively influenced many of the people in his town. It was a movie with a good moral but with a slightly distorted understanding of the role and function of heavenly angels.

Clarence was a second-class angel who needed to earn his wings, which is not biblical. Clarence was able to help create the illusion that George had not existed, which good angels do not do to accomplish their mission. This was not a New Age portrayal of angel activity on earth like we have today, but it was a beginning of raising spurious angel consciousness and awareness in society.

2. *The Preacher's Wife*

Denzel Washington, as the angel Dudley in *The Preacher's Wife*, falls out of heaven into the snow-covered front yard of a minister whose church is floundering and whose marriage is withering. Sent to help the minister, Dudley, in the process, falls in love with the preacher's wife. The movie is entertaining, but portrays heavenly angels as interacting in human affairs to the extent of having human feelings and even succumbing to the temptation of coveting and romancing another man's wife. In the end, Dudley returns to heaven, leaving things in order, but clearly leaving the audience with another distorted view of heavenly angels and their earthly involvement with humans.

3. *Michael*

In the movie *Michael,* John Travolta, an angel appearing in human disguise, displayed some of the most crude and immoral human characteristics. Michael is depicted as a beer-guzzling, womanizing, intemperate slob. These characteristics, plus his disgusting eating habits and unkempt personal appearance had even the hardened cynics in the movie blinking in disbelief. However, in the end, when he selflessly gives up part of his own divine life force in order to bring a friend's pet back to life, his friends' sympathy and admiration are regained and angels are once again held in high esteem.

The Christian can be confused by such a portrayal of angels. Michael (which, by the way, is the name for Jesus Christ the Archangel in the Bible) portrays an angel with morals and behavior that is substandard even by human guidelines. Trying to match the biblical concept of angels with the "angel" such as portrayed by Travolta can cause either revulsion (such as the author experienced) or a new paradigm regarding the realm and role of heavenly beings, which may just be the reaction desired by the producers.

Travolta's portrayal of Michael should be revolting to all Christians if they stop to think who the biblical Michael really is and what His function is. His name alone in Hebrew literally means "who is like God?" Christ is Michael (Rev. 12:7). Michael is mentioned five times in the Bible. And every time He's mentioned, He is defending the saints from their foes or fighting the dragon. The book of Daniel mentions Michael three times (Daniel 10:13, Daniel 10:21, and Daniel 12:1 where he's called the "great prince" who defends the people of Israel. The fourth time Michael is mentioned is in Jude 9 where He appears as the archangel who disputes with the devil over the body of Moses. The last mention is made in Revelation 12:7 where Michael and his angels fought and defeated the Devil and his angels and cast them out of heaven down to earth.

The biblical Michael, is the leader of the heavenly host of angels. To have a character using one of the names of our Saviour and portraying Him in the movies as uncouth and immoral should be very offensive to Christians. I wonder what the Hindus and the Buddhists would do if Hollywood would portray Shiva, Hare Krishna, Buddha, or even the Dalai Lama characterized in a sacrilegious manner the way they did with the angel in *Michael*? You know what they would do. They would protest, bitterly protest. They would not take it sitting down, eating popcorn, as we have done.

Angels and TV

Long before TV viewers were *Touched by an Angel* or told about the *Promised Land*, the TV angel movement phenomenon was paved by Michael Landon's role in *Highway to Heaven*. All three of the programs portray angels as being eager to do good and wonderful deeds for people without ever involving God, Christ, or the Holy Spirit. When the name of God is mentioned, it's just a happenstance. What these programs are doing is meeting the demand for angel consciousness, contact, and work with a distorted role and function of genuine heavenly angels.

1. *Highway to Heaven*

It is true that many of the episodes in this program are moral, "innocent," uplifting, and well meaning, but what they are also doing is introducing TV viewers to false biblical concepts of heavenly angel intervention with humans, not to mention the false doctrines slipped in from time to time. For instance, in one of the episodes of

Highway to Heaven, the country preacher, on Sunday morning is addressing his local congregation (with Michael Landon present) with these words, "We are not here to judge, but to serve. You don't have to believe in God to go to heaven. You just have to do 'good.' God is not looking for recognition." The first sentence may be true, but the other three are blatantly false and misleading. This is definitely New Age thinking.

2. *Touched by an Angel*

Streetwise Tess (Della Reese) and her band of angels in an episode of *Touched by an Angel* apply "tough love," as they untangle the lives of individuals in a mess or in deep trouble. It is so unreal to think that angels can occupy positions in our society such as social workers at a city agency or at other establishments for days at a time, interacting constantly with human beings, at all levels, and then disappear with no one even missing them. In another episode, God made Monica, one of the angels, temporarily blind so she could accept people as they are and not be prejudiced by their color. This is so far out in left field to think that some heavenly beings are "racists" or need to learn lessons about color and race issues.

Part of the danger in viewing TV series like this is that you tend to drop your guard as you conclude in your mind that "finally" here is a wholesome TV program that teaches "Christian morals." Ellen White tells us not to be off guard for a moment.[181] We must be discerning and always on guard against what we allow to enter our minds through the five senses, because what we accept into our minds either strengthens or undermines our Christian faith. And remember, true heavenly angels will never teach anything contrary to revealed truth as it is found in God's holy Word.

3. *Promised Land*

In one of the episodes of *Promised Land,* Dinah, the young daughter, kept seeing Andrew, the "angel of death," on the side of the highway. She began to fear that one of her loved ones was going to die. She kept telling her father, "I just know something terrible is going to happen." Sure enough, the Greenes were involved in an auto accident and a young woman was seriously injured. Dinah confided to her father that she believed that because of everything that had been happening to them that God "was out to get us." When Dinah met the "angel of death" outside the hospital chapel she asked him, "Did you come for Jennifer?"

He said, "No, I came for you." When she looked at him quizzically, he said, "I don't always come to take people to heaven. Sometimes I come to bring heaven to them. God sent me to tell you that He's very proud to have you as His daughter."

The so-called "angel of death" does not come to earth to take people to heaven. When people die, the Bible teaching is that they stay dead until they are called forth in one of the resurrections (Rev. 20:5, 6; 1 Thess. 4:13-16).

The subtle danger in the angel TV programs is that they are perceived as good, wholesome, family viewing. I'm sure that most Christian churches would approve them as something people could safely watch. And this is exactly what the enemy of our souls has planned—to disarm Christians by allowing them to think that they can drop their mental defenses and sit unsuspectingly through the whole program.

Ellen White says that error cannot stand alone.[182] What these angel imposters do is take a thread of truth and weave it into a lie. There is so much "good" in the programs that people don't question the false concepts expressed such as the different ways heavenly angels intervene in human lives.

Angel seminar

On one of my recent trips to Southern California, I saw an advertisement on TV for a seminar on angels. Since I was planning to write on angels, I decided to find out what these people were teaching. As it turned out, the seminar was sponsored by Elizabeth Clare Prophet, who is a New Ager. At 7:30 that evening, I arrived at the five-star hotel in Pasadena, California, where the seminar was to be held. Realizing the spiritual danger in which I might be placing myself, I decided to get a seat close to the door just in case I needed to get out of there in a hurry. I really didn't know what to expect.

There were about 45 people in the room, casually dressed and seated on chairs facing the raised platform. The back of the room had some books, videos and other angel stuff for sale. The attendees, who had to pay $15.00 each, were men and women ranging from college age to adults in their late fifties. The evening lecturer, a thin man in his mid forties, dressed in a dark brown pin-striped business suit, was just starting to introduce the subject for the evening when I arrived.

As I had planned, there was an empty seat right next to the double doors which opened into the seminar room. I quickly sat down in it and sent a silent prayer upward. I took a pad of paper out of my pocket to jot down some notes. Later on, when things got too uncomfortable, I began writing out my prayer on the pad, asking God to protect me and keep the speaker from noticing that I was not "with it." At one time, I came close to leaving when the speaker began to lead the angel seekers in audible chants that steadily increased, both in volume and rapidity. The whole room began to fill up with a mystical and mysterious sound. This must have been the high point of the whole meeting, because soon after this the chanting subsided and the speaker returned to his lecture, speaking in normal tones.

False teachings about angels

Essentially, what this particular seminar taught was that there are seven archangels that correspond to the seven rays of light, or better known to New Agers as the seven Hindu Chakra energy areas and their corresponding colors. For example: "Archangel Michael and Faith" supposedly provide protection for travelers and correspond to the Throat-Chakra Meditation, which is marked with a blue glowing color. When a person wants to contact "Michael," there are a number of invocations, prayers, meditations, hymns, decrees, and mantras to assist him in doing so. Most of the mantras used in a booklet describing the seven archangels were in Hindi. There was even a Hindi song dedicated to Lord Krishna.

The Fifth Ray of Light, which is green in color, corresponds to the Hindu "Third-eye Chakra," and is called Archangel Raphael and Mother Mary. As you would guess, it has a "ballad" or song dedicated to The Virgin of Guadalupe (the patron saint of Mexico) and ends with a good portion of the Catholic rosary "Hail, Mary, full of grace!"[183]

One of the problems with angel seminars of this type is that they are laden with Eastern mysticism and therefore out of harmony with what the Bible says about holy angels. For example, the Scriptures only mention one archangel, not seven. Another problem is that these seven archangels are connected with the Hindu chakra energy centers of light, which are pagan and occult.

On the back page of a booklet I purchased at the seminar, entitled, "Angels, Angels, Angels" by Elizabeth Clare Prophet is a reading entitled, "God's Real in Me." It ends with a Coda which reads;

I'm glad that I'm me,

I'm glad that I'm real,

I'm glad that I AM really God.[184]

By now, of course, you realize that this seminar was very much New Age. The teaching that we are God, or gods, is one of the tenets of the New Age movement. But let's take a look now at the person behind the seminar—Elizabeth Clare Prophet.

Elizabeth Clare Prophet

Elizabeth Clare Wulf (Prophet was her first husband's surname) was born in 1939 in Red Bank, New Jersey, and is considered one of the foremost authorities on The Ascended Masters and pseudo-angelology. By the age of 18 she had read the complete works of Mary Baker Eddy, along with her Bible. For a time she attended the local Christian Science church. However, longing for a greater and deeper experience of truth and metaphysics, she continued her search. Mrs. Prophet believes that "the concept of the incarnation of the Light of God, the inner Buddha and the inner Christ, is what has been taken from us in the West in church, in synagogue, in mosque, in temple."[185]

Since 1961, Elizabeth Clare Prophet has called herself a "pioneer of modern religious thought." She teaches the mystical paths of the world's major religions infused with fire of the Holy Spirit and the Age of Aquarius." Her students call her, "Guru Ma" (the teacher who represents the Divine Mother). She also claims to be a prophet for God and the messenger for the Ascended Masters.[186]

Prophet believes that Jesus, at the age of 12, went to Tibet and lived there until He was 29, mastering the ancient Tibetan and Hindu scriptures.[187]

She is the leader of the Church Universal and Triumphant, whose headquarters are located on an exquisite 28,000-acre Royal Teton ranch in Wyoming, bordering Yellowstone National Park. She claims to have spent the early years of her life, until the age of 22, searching for the teachings of the Ascended Masters. When she found them, she devoted herself to the spreading of that message.[188] Mrs. Prophet refers to the teachings of the Ascended Masters as "Ancient wisdom for the New Age."[189] Her books include New Age best-sellers *The Lost Years of Jesus*, *Saint Germain on Alchemy*, and *The Human Aura*.

There's no question but that Mrs. Prophet is definitely a very influential "prophet" of the New Age with an alluring message of deception. Her teachings on angels are a gross misrepresentation and distortion of the mission of God's holy angels. The angels of God only intervene in the lives of humans to do God's bidding, not ours. They are not our servants. They are God's messengers to protect and influence us for good.

Danger in contacting angels

When people begin communicating with their "guardian angel," there's a strong possibility that in time this "spiritual being" will replace the authority and worship of God in their lives because this so-called angel is supplying them with all their spiritual needs, inquiries and guidance or direction for their life. Following an angel also requires little faith because instead of faith, you rely on intuition, feelings, images and mystical experiences. When you make a request of God, you must have a faith that requires patience, heart searching and obedience, trusting Him to do what is right for your life.

There is also a false sense of power that comes from believing that you have tapped into the esoteric spiritual knowledge (gnosis) of your guardian angel. In a time when a person feels things are out of control in their life, this access to supernatural knowledge and power seems to be just what is needed. It offers a way out, a means to controlling their own destiny, putting them in the driver's seat.

Angels and the New Age movement

The recent "angel movement" has been embraced and nurtured by the New Age/New Spirituality movement. It has become part of the New Age movement because angel contact, angel consciousness, and angel work are natural and logical extensions of the modern phenomenon of channeling universal entities or spirits. Although this spurious type of communication is prohibited in the Bible (Deuteronomy 18:10-12), New Age theology teaches that contacting "angels" is not spiritualism, but rather communication with divine beings.

With all this hype about angels, we Christians need to be reminded of the malicious and subtle workings of the millions of evil angels in our world whose only delight is misery and destruction. For this reason God has appointed a guardian angel to every follower of Christ to watch and shield us from the power of Satan and his evil angels. *The Great Controversy* states that these evil ones have "leagued together for the dishonor of God and the destruction of man."[190] Some would like to ignore this fact, but ignoring it won't make it go away. In fact, to deny the existence and intent of evil angels is very dangerous. According to the *Great Controversy:* "None are in greater danger from the influence of evil spirits than those who, notwithstanding the direct and ample testimony of the Scriptures, deny the existence and agency of the devil and his angels."[191]

It is comforting to know that "The angel of the Lord encampeth round about them that fear him, and delivereth them" Psalm 34:7. And the servant of the Lord echoes the same promise: "The wicked one cannot break through the guard which God has stationed about His people."[192]

One of the great dangers in trying to develop a New Age angel consciousness is that in time prayer and the Bible are made of no effect. Interaction with "angels" can also negate the need for dependence on God and put further distance between man and the true Mediator Jesus Christ. New Age theology says we live in a benign universe where all you have to do is ask an angel for help. If that is the case, why wait on God, Christ and the Holy Spirit when you can talk directly to an "angel"?

Deceived by angels

Take the case of Sharon Lee and Debra Halstead who joined a group of Adventists who were receiving messages and spiritual gifts from who they thought were heavenly angels sent from God. These two sisters, who are fourth-generation Adventists, were totally deceived by demonic angels masquerading as heavenly angels who told Sharon and Debra to kill six people because they were "totaled" or "demon-possessed." They succeeded in killing two, and now they're in the Oregon penitentiary for women.[193]

Biblical teachings of angels

Today it seems most people who are interested in angels are obtaining information from every place except the true source. The Bible and the Spirit of Prophecy have a wealth of information on the nature, purpose, and role of angels—both good and evil.

The Hebrew word for angels is *mal'ak* and the Greek word is *aggelos.* Both mean "messenger." Angels are supernatural beings, "created by God, superior to man, and acting as a representative or messenger of God."[194] They interact with people to do God's bidding.

Sometimes *aggelos* and *mal'ak* refer to humans, as in Mark 1:2, where it applies to John the Baptist since he was Christ's messenger. "Behold, I send my messenger (*aggelos*) before Your face. And in Malachi 3:1, which is the prophecy of the mission of John the Baptist: "Behold, I will send my messenger." For this reason, one needs to look at the context of the Bible passages to determine whether "messenger" is referring to a human or to a celestial being.

The word *angel* appears in the Bible 300 times, in at least 24 of its books. They are also referred to as *cherubim, seraphs,* and *ministering spirits,* etc. It would be good to remember that there are twice as many good angels as there are bad angels.[195] The Bible writers describe the company of angels in heaven as "ten thousand times ten thousand and thousands of thousands" and "an innumerable company" (Daniel 7:10; Hebrews 12:22).

Only three names of angels in the Bible are recorded: Michael, Gabriel, and Lucifer. I wonder if this is not because if we knew their names there would be a great temptation to worship or render homage to them. Catholics have a saint for each day of the year and good Catholic parents, in addition to the given names, also give their children the name of their birthday saint.

Billions of angels

There must be billions of angels because we are told that every person in this world has an angel assigned to him, to guard him and to lead him to Christ.

> When the earthborn children know it not, they have angels of light as their companions. A silent witness guards every soul that lives, seeking to draw that soul to Christ. As long as there is hope, until men resist the Holy Spirit to their eternal ruin, they are guarded by heavenly intelligences.[196]

So when men irrevocably reject the Holy Spirit, they are left to the mercy of evil angels who influence and control their lives.

Everyone who accepts Christ has a guardian angel: "A guardian angel is appointed to every follower of Christ. These heavenly watchers shield the righteous from the power of the wicked one."[197]

By contrast, evil angels work against the people of this earth for their eternal destruction.

> Evil spirits, in the beginning created sinless, were equal in nature, power, and glory with the holy beings that are now God's messengers. But fallen through sin, they are leagued together for the dishonor of God and the destruction of men. United with Satan in his rebellion, and with him cast out from heaven, they have, through all succeeding ages, co-operated with him in his warfare against the divine authority. We are told in Scripture of their confederacy and government, of their various orders, of their intelligence and subtlety, and of their malicious designs against the peace and happiness of men.[198]

The war in heaven

The Bible tells us in Revelation 12:7-9 that there was a war in heaven and that Michael, the archangel, who is Christ, and His loyal angels fought against the dragon, (Satan, originally known as Lucifer) and the rebellious angels. Lucifer and his angels lost and were exiled from heaven, cast down to earth. That's why the apostle Paul in Ephesians 6 reminds the believers that our major warfare here on earth between good and evil is not against flesh and blood or humans. But rather "against the principalities, against powers, against the rulers of the darkness of this world, against spiritual wickedness in high places" (Eph. 6:12).

Satan and his evil angels are bent on destroying the human race now and for eternity. The fallen angels themselves hate us so much because when the great controversy is over and we are taken to heaven, we will fill the places that the fallen angels vacated.

The Bible gives many incidences of angels intervening in the lives of people, but it is always God directing this activity. Humans are only the recipients of the heaven-sent messengers of God. We have many examples of this in Scripture, such as Genesis 18, where the three angels (one of which was Christ) visited Abraham, to prepare him for the destruction of Sodom. In Chapter 19, we see the two angels coming to Lot's house to take them out of Sodom.

The angel Gabriel announces to the virgin Mary that she is going to give birth to the Son of God (Luke 1:26-38). Gabriel, along with other angels, was sent to minister to Christ in His darkest hour in the Garden of Gethsemane.[199]

The apostle Paul also mentions that sometimes we entertain angels without realizing it (Hebrews 13:2). And many stories abound about angels touching the lives of people, especially Christians. Perhaps you have also experienced once or twice what you believed was an angel that briefly stepped in and out of your life.

Biblical criteria for angels

I want to remind you that in the last days the activity of demonic angels will increase. If you are having, or have had, an encounter with what you believe to be a holy angel, perhaps these biblical criteria could serve to keep you from being deceived by Satan and his evil angels:

1. First of all we should bear in mind that in the great controversy there are two kinds of angels actively involved in the affairs of humans—good angels and evil angels. Both have supernatural powers to perform miracles (Rev. 16:14) and occasionally appear in human form. Therefore, we need to pray that God, through the Bible and His Holy Spirit, will help us discern which is which.

2. Heavenly angels are sent by God to do His bidding and not our own. In other words, they are not here so that we can utilize them to gain insights (esoteric knowledge) or special favors from them. Angels of God have been sent here mainly to protect us from the evil one and his fallen angels, the demons (Psalm 34:7). "The angels are with us every day, to guard and protect us from the assaults of the enemy."[200]

3. Heavenly angels do not bring "new light" that contradicts the word of God (Isaiah 8:20; Acts 17:11; 2 Timothy 3:15-17). No matter how beautiful the experience with so-called "heavenly beings" or empirical encounters, they are not to take the place of or supercede a "thus saith the Lord."

4. Beware of anyone who claims to have the "gift" of speaking with angels or channeling them. These people are generally those who feel that they have a closer relationship with the Lord and who tend to disregard or make of little effect the leadership of God's established church on earth and share their knowledge with just a few chosen ones. "By their fruits ye shall know them" (Matt. 7:20).

5. Even though these spurious angels speak words of truth, be not deceived by the misrepresentations and subtle insinuations of doubt that they cast on the Scriptures and God's church on earth. Be discerning of the sly introduction of paranormal, metaphysical teachings, such as out-of- -body experiences (astral projections), near-death experiences, and the existence of universal entities (spirits) who want to guide and prosper your life.

Increased activity of angels in the last days

As we draw close to the end of time, there will be increased manifestations of evil angels' activity with humans here on earth. Satan's deceptions will escalate greatly. The servant of the Lord says:

> The coming of the Lord is to be preceded by "the working of Satan with all power and signs and lying wonders, and with all deceivableness of unrighteousness" (2 Thess. 2:9,10). And the apostle John, describing the miracle-working power that will be manifested in the last days, declares: "He doeth great wonders, so that he maketh fire come down from heaven on the earth in the sight of men, and deceiveth them that dwell on the earth by the means of those miracles which he had power to do" (Revelation 13:13, 14). No mere impostures are here foretold. Men are deceived by the miracles which Satan's agents have power to do, not which they pretend to do.[201]

This will include all kinds of deceptions, including Satan's agents or evil angels appearing as heavenly angels, but eventually leading people to eternal destruction. Some of these increased spiritualistic manifestations in the time of the end will also include evil angels appearing as our deceased loved ones to deceive us. "Spiritualism is the masterpiece of deception" of Satan, Ellen White says.

> It is Satan's most successful and fascinating delusion—one calculated to take hold of the sympathies of those who have laid their loved ones in the grave. Evil angels come in the form of those loved ones, and relate incidents connected with their lives, and perform acts which they performed while living. In this way they lead persons to believe that their dead friends are angels, hovering over them and communicating with them. These evil angels, who assume to be the deceased friends, are regarded with a certain idolatry, and with many their word has greater weight than the Word of God."[202]

But just as the deceptions of Satan and his angels increase in the close of this world's history, we should increase our study of God's

Word. Our prayer life should include the constant request for God's protection from all evil influences in our lives. The conflict will be severe. Everyone's faith will be tested. But Ellen White says:

> If we do what we can on our part to be ready for the conflict that is just before us, God will do His part, and His all-powerful arm will protect us. He would sooner send every angel out of glory to make a hedge about faithful souls, than have them deceived and led away by the lying wonders of Satan.[203]

Pray for discernment

The present increased interest in angel contact, angel consciousness, and angel work among New Agers and Christians alike should cause every sincere follower of Christ to study and understand for himself the true nature and mission of God's heavenly angels. The doctrine of angels is one of the most comforting teachings the Bible extends to believers, for they are our faithful and constant allies to help us in the struggle of good and evil. But as with everything else, these good angels have their counterparts whose only purpose for existence is to deceive and destroy every member of the human race. May God help us to be able to discern between the angels of light and the angels of darkness, between the friends or foes.

9

The Lure of New Age Holistic Health/Medicine

The growing popularity of alternative New Age medicine

Thirty years ago hardly anyone had heard the term *holistic health*, much less *New Age holistic health*. Today, however, *New Age holistic health*, *New Age medicine*, *alternative medicine*, *integrative medicine*, and *body/mind medicine* have become household words. For many, they have become viable alternatives to conventional health care and medicine. But no matter what title is given to these alternative New Age therapies and remedies, they form one of the broadest entry pathways into the New Age movement.

Some of the expressed reasons for this trend are that conventional medicine has become too costly, too impersonal, and too drug and surgery oriented. People today are turning to the so-called "natural" and non-invasive alternative health/medicine therapies and practices (most of which are New Age) as opposed to pharmaceutical, chemically produced drugs and surgery. Also, they want to participate in and be more "in command" of their healing process.

In addition, New Age physicians or practitioners generally tend to take a more personal interest in their patients. Holistic health doctors treat the spiritual, emotional, and physical dimensions of their patients along with their physical symptoms, which patients greatly appreciate.

Gale and a New Age doctor referral

Some people wind up being treated by New Age doctors without realizing it simply because friends or a referral service recommend them. Gale was suffering with an abdominal pain. She called an association's telephone referral service that recommended James Berry, who turned out to be a New Age doctor. When she entered his crowded clinic waiting room, she was pleased to learn from other patients that her new doctor was going to treat her whole person—body, mind, and spirit. Dr. Berry told her that she had hypoglycemia, a pre-diabetic condition that could be controlled by diet alone. But diet alone did not help. In the course of nine years, her New Age doctor recommended castor oil packs applied to the abdomen and acupuncture. When her condition worsened, instead of sending her to a specialist, he referred her to an astrology center to have her astrological chart read. The mention of astrology was a red flag to her. She gave up on that doctor and finally saw a gynecologist who quickly discovered the cause of her growing pain and removed a grapefruit-sized, blood-filled cyst. She was lucky. Others have not been as fortunate.

Holistic health can become of even more interest to people who have terminal diseases or medical problems for which conventional medical doctors have no cures. In desperation the patient begins to explore alternative medicine and therapies without realizing the physical and spiritual dangers involved.

Naisbitt's forecast for New Age medicine

In 1982, America's *Megatrends* mogul, John Naisbitt, a New Age believer, wrote, "America's loss of faith in the medical establishment gave a strong symbolic push to the paradigm shift from institutional help to self-help."[204] Naisbitt forecasted this medical self-help paradigm shift in part as being from "the medical establishment's program of annual physical exams, drugs and surgery," to a "wealth of new-age remedies—acupuncture, acupressure, vitamin therapy, charismatic faith healing and preventive health care through diet and exercise."[205] It should be noted that New Age holistic health is a mixed bag and that Naisbitt's regimen of New Age remedies includes areas of health care that may not be specifically New Age, depending on what they consist of, such as some vitamin therapies, diet, and exercise.

Naisbitt's predictions, however, have become a reality in the '90s. *Time*'s cover story, in its November 4, 1991, issue, entitled "Why New Age Medicine Is Catching On," stated that "the growth of alternative medicine, now a $27 billion-a-year industry, is more than just an American flirtation with exotic New Age thinking. It reflects a gnawing dissatisfaction with conventional, or allopathic medicine."[206]

Two personalities in the medical profession that are popularizing New Age integrative medicine and helping to revolutionize the way we look at health care and medicine are Dr. Deepak Chopra and Dr. Andrew Weil. *Time* Magazine called Chopra "The Emperor of the Soul." Chopra combines conventional medicine with Indian metaphysics, "telling Americans where spirit and body interact."[207] Chopra has captured the attention of many Hollywood celebrities like Demi Moore.

Weil, a Harvard graduate, who spent several years in South America studying shamanism,[208] now is a prime promoter of New Age remedies and considers himself a guru in these health care alternatives. *Time* magazine called him a "medicine man" who had made New Age remedies popular.[209] At the time of this writing, Weil has a daily column on Time-Warner's Pathfinder Internet page, and from a link on his page, web browsers can go to a site where they can hear him speak. One week recently the audio portion consisted of Dr. Weil leading listeners through a relaxation meditation accompanied by the music of New Age composer Stephen Halpern. Weil's remedies include Eastern meditation, acupuncture, hypnotism, and cranial manipulation.[210]

The popularity of New Age Alternative therapies has prompted many national insurance companies (such as Aetna, U.S. Health, American National, CIGNA Health Care, Great West Life Insurance, John Alden Life, Kaiser Permanente, Mutual of Omaha, New England Mutual Life, Prudential, and UniCare, etc.) to cover New Age alternative therapies such as acupuncture, biofeedback, and homeopathy.[211] Many regional insurance companies, such as New York Life and American Western Life, are doing the same.

Oxford Health Plans was the first major health insurer in the

United States to offer a program of alternative medical coverage to its 1.4 million members. Their network includes acupuncturists, massage therapists, chiropractors, dietitians, nutritionists, yoga instructors, and naturopathic physicians. "We decided to take this step," says Hassan Rifaat, M.D., manager of the program, "after polling our members and learning that one third were already using alternative therapies, while 75 percent were interested in doing so. It was also an area that employers wanted us to move into."[212]

The New England Journal of Medicine in January of 1993 stated that one in three Americans were using unconventional medicine. One of these is Shirley MacLaine, dancer, actress, and author, who is probably one of the best recognized New Age celebrities. She believes so much in the so-called "natural" holistic approach that she reported in her 1985 book *Dancin' in the Light* that she no longer had a family physician. Instead, she utilizes quartz crystals, Hindu mantras, visualizing, and meditation.

Defining New Age medicine

In my study of alternative New Age holistic health therapies, I have concluded that that these therapies can be recognized by several characteristics that they hold in common:

(1) Their origins are linked to pagan and occult worldviews and philosophies;

(2) They are embraced by the New Age movement because they share the same philosophy and ideology;

(3) They do not function according to the physiological and anatomical structure and function of the body;

(4) They have a strong emphasis on the metaphysical (the realm of the spirits).

There are as many as 120 alternative New Age holistic health therapies, generally falling into five categories:

(1) energy manipulation (acupuncture, acupressure, Shiatsu, therapeutic touch, reflexology)

(2) mind-body medicine (yoga, transcendental meditation, guided imagery, visualization, biofeedback, hypnosis)

(3) divination (pendulum divination, "applied" kinesiology, iridology, aura readings)

(4) the supernatural (channeling, psychic healing, chakra balancing)

(5) so-called "natural" remedies (homeopathy, aromatherapy)

New Age alternative medicine movement continues to evolve

The proliferation of health food stores that promote New Age holistic health books and remedies and New Age holistic health clinics and practitioners throughout the nation is helping to make holistic health perhaps the fastest growing phenomenon of the New Age movement. As is the case with the New Age movement, New Age holistic health continues to evolve and develop, notwithstanding the lack of a central organization, according to Dr. Paul C. Reisser, a Christian family physician in Thousand Oaks, California, and co-author of *New Age Medicine.*

The holistic health movement at present defies simple definition. It is not represented by any single organization, group, or type of practice, and it is continually being reshaped by its adherents. These include physicians and scientists with impressive credentials, chiropractors and osteopaths, psychologists and sociologists, healers and mystics, nurses and lay people, as well as an odd assortment of health "practitioners" whose ideas and techniques have varying degrees of credibility.[213]

Sharing the same ideology

The reason Alternative New Age medicine therapies and practices are called "New Age" is that they share the same philosophical ideology (nonbiblical worldviews) and goals (self-awareness and transformation). J. Gordon Melton, co-author of *The New Age Almanac*, notes that it was during the 1970s that

> The New Age movement and the holistic health movement merged to the extent that it is difficult, if not impossible, for an observer to draw the line between them. It is apparent that *they share ideology*. It is equally apparent that New Age spokespersons look to the holistic health

movement as *a major component of their movement,* and
the holistic health practitioners look to the New Agers
both for public support and as the clientele upon whom
they practice their profession (italics added).[214]

The philosophical goals

Of equal concern are the underlying goals of the New Age holistic health practitioners—to introduce to their patients a new paradigm or way of thinking. Dr. Reisser says that

New Agers are far less interested in reforming the way health care is
provided than they are in changing the worldview of its patients. The
importance of this fact cannot be overstated. Beneath the appealing
concern for healing the total person—body, mind and spirit—lies a
compulsion to bring radical change to the way we view all of life.[215]

This is why Marilyn Ferguson refers to New Agers as "Aquarian
Conspirators." No matter what profession the New Ager may have,
his overriding purpose, his hidden agenda, his cause to champion is
to get others to accept a new paradigm and worldview philosophy.

The New Age in one word: Transformation

If the whole New Age movement were boiled down to one word,
it would be "transformation," personal and social. This transformation involves a new paradigm, the "hidden picture" as Marilyn
Ferguson puts it. It involves transformation from the old way of
thinking to a new way of thinking; from a conscious state to an
altered state of consciousness and self-awareness; from traditional
values to new values. Many elements of this new paradigm make it a
nonbiblical worldview.

One of the prominent means for accomplishing the desired transformation is healing through the methods of alternative holistic
health, which is possibly the single most identifiable segment of the
New Age movement.

J. Gordon Melton, author of the *New Age Encyclopedia,* says that

The central vision of the New Age is one of radical
transformation. On an individual level that experience is

very personal and mystical. It involves an awakening of a new reality of self—such as a discovery of psychic abilities, the experience of a physical or psychological healing, the emergence of new potentials within oneself, an intimate experience within a community, or the acceptance of a new picture of the universe.[216]

The New Age Almanac addresses the New Age holistic health movement, by stating that:

Transformation, as often as not, comes in the form of healing—*healing of the body*, mind, relationships, or the effects of spiritual traumas. *Healings* have often been experienced at the hands of unorthodox healing modalities and often after the failure of physicians of the more culturally accepted variety, be they medical doctors or psychiatrists. As the New Age movement developed, it accepted into itself a concurrently developing movement that was taking a new look at traditional alternative healing arts and the possibility of treating conditions with which orthodox medicine and Freudian psychiatry were having the most difficulty. Many of these alternative medicines had *a common ideological base and shared common beliefs with the New Age movement, hence their merger seemed logical.*[217] (italics added)

Marilyn Ferguson and Kenneth Pelletier (author of *Holistic Medicine*, which promulgates the Eastern concept of holistic healing) affirm that "illness . . . is potentially transformative because it can cause a sudden shift in values, an awakening."[218]

Ferguson ties holistic health to the New Age concept of greater self-awareness and transformation.

For many Aquarian Conspirators, an involvement in health care was a major stimulus to transformation. Just as the search for self becomes a search for health, so the pursuit of health can lead to greater self-awareness. All wholeness is the same. The proliferating holistic health centers and networks have drawn many into the consciousness movement. A nurse said, "If healing becomes a reality with you, it's a lifestyle. Altered states of consciousness accompany it, increase telepathy. It's an adventure."[219]

Any serious illness can cause a person to do some in-depth thinking about spirituality, personal values, and the meaning of life and death. During this experience, a person can become distressed and desperate, making him or her vulnerable to nonconventional and questionable therapies and treatments for wellness. Cognizant of this fact, New Age holistic health practitioners, whether physicians or lay persons, are eager to take naive, unsuspecting patients into their care and in time introduce them to the underlying philosophies and beliefs of the New Age movement. Thus New Age alternative medicine and holistic health can become entryways or pathways into the New Age movement, many times without the patient's even realizing it.

Holistic health—the entry point

Former New Age priest and author Will Baron's own testimony of how he came into the New Age movement speaks volumes:

Even though I had been brought up in a Christian family that attended church each week, I was still deceived by the New Age movement's promises of *health*, happiness, and fulfillment. I was completely led astray, eventually becoming totally immersed in the world of the occult.

For example, my own active involvement with the New Age movement began when I joined a London-based international networking organization called "Health for the New Age." Not even knowing what the term "New Age" meant, I wasn't looking for spirit guides or occult practices. I was simply interested in finding information about *alternative healing techniques* for a condition that I had (italics added).[220]

The book that changed Will Baron from a Seventh-day Adventist to a New Age occultist was *Stress Disease* by psychotherapist Peter Blythe. In Will's own words, "The power of a book can be phenomenal."[221]

Baron was looking only for "*healing*, meaning, and harmony" in his life. Blythe's book introduced him to the New Age "holistic" concept—the idea that mind, body, and spirit are integral components of an individual and that in order to have health, all must be in harmony, a concept shared by Christians as well. However, when New Agers speak of "spirit," they are referring to an immortal, mystical "spirit," or "soul" associated with out-of-the-body experiences and reincarnation. Baron continues:

> The idea of "*holistic health*" sounded appealing. The concept of a necessary balance between body, mind, and spirit made sense. I thought, Maybe I can pick up some good advice and pass it on to my friends. The last few chapters presented information on "*alternative therapy*" techniques for common diseases. Being familiar only with surgery and medication, I was fascinated to read of therapies such as *acupuncture, homeopathy, psychic surgery, chakra balancing, rebirthing, primal therapy, reiki, crystals, and bioenergetics.* Descriptions of these treatments talked a lot about "energies," "balance," and "wholeness" (italics added).[222]

> It was the first time I had ever heard of the term "New Age." I had no idea what it meant. I wasn't interested in getting involved in the occult; I was simply searching for better health and for contentment. *Stress Disease* mentioned a London-based organization called "Health for the New Age." Wanting to learn more about these alternative healing practices, I joined it and arranged to have a meeting with its founder.[223]

For Baron, that was the beginning of a twelve-year journey into the occult world of the New Age movement.

A different kind of revolution

In her book, *The Aquarian Conspiracy,* Marilyn Ferguson speaks of New Agers as conspirators and revolutionaries involved in the Aquarian Conspiracy, which is a "different kind of revolution."[224] To see that it is a revolution, one needs only to read the literature of the movement or attend its meetings to discover a distinct, mystical worldview foreign to that of biblical Christianity. It is a worldview that encompasses

> *"New Consciousness,"* a loose synthesis of various el-

ements of mysticism, occultism, spiritism and animism, combined with concepts derived from modern paranormal research (i.e., parapsychology) and from the experiences of those who have experienced altered states of consciousness. Sometimes referred to as the human potential movement, the New Consciousness represents a sort of supernatural/psychic humanism which strives to bring about a radical transformation of thinking in society at large. The result, we are told, will be a New Age, referred to variously as the "Age of Enlightenment," the "Age of Aquarius," and other titles. *Holistic health is, in essence, the banner under which the New Consciousness is making its move into the realm of health and medicine* (italics added).[225]

Adventist wholistic health

New Age holistic health/medicine can be confusing to a Seventh-day Adventist because historically the Church, almost from its inception, has had its own alternative health practices with a philosophy of "wholism" or "wholeness"—treating the whole person and not just pain, disease, and symptoms. Even though there are some members who practice or participate in some forms of New Age holistic health, knowingly or unknowingly, neither the Bible nor the writings of Ellen G. White support or espouse any of the alternative New Age therapies.

Differences between the Seventh-day Adventist wholistic health philosophy and the New Age holistic health philosophy include:

1. The Adventist philosophy is undergirded and supported by a biblical theistic worldview, in which God is the only sovereign Creator and Sustainer of the universe and everything in it. In New Age holistic health, there is a blending of nonbiblical worldviews, such as monism, pantheism, animism, etc.

2. The ultimate aim of Seventh-day Adventist wholistic health philosophy is to make man whole, that is, to restore him to the image of his Creator. The goal of New Age holistic health philosophy is

to transform man to a new paradigm of seeing himself as a demi-god and as a body-mind self-healer.

3. Seventh-day Adventist wholistic health philosophy teaches that humanity should depend on God for life and healing, whereas New Age holistic health teaches a dependence on mystical energies and self.

Holistic health, the right arm of the New Age movement

Just as health reform among Seventh-day Adventists is "the right arm of the third angel's message,"[226] so is holistic health to the New Age movement. As the medical missionary work serves as an opening wedge for the Adventist gospel, holistic health opens the door to the New Age movement. It is one of the major entry points or pathways into the New Age movement that Marilyn Ferguson referred to in her book. This is why New Age holistic medicine is spiritually dangerous. It is subtle and deceiving because it is passed off as "natural" and "holistic."

The spiritual danger

New Age holistic health/medicine is spiritually dangerous because, if its therapies and treatments work, it can create a bond of trust between the New Age practitioner and the patient, which can make him or her susceptible to the teachings and philosophies of the New Age that the practitioners introduce.

Because this danger of being drawn unsuspectingly into the New Age is very real, it is imperative that we become aware of the danger and how to avoid it.

10

Traditional Chinese Medicine, Including Acupuncture

Tracing the roots of New Age holistic health

The roots of the New Age holistic health movement can be traced back to the ancient philosophical and religious beliefs of China, India, and Egypt. Reviewing these roots reveals that they are deeply embedded in the fertile soil of the Eastern mystical religions of Hinduism, Buddhism, Taoism, and other pagan and occult beliefs which subscribe to nonbiblical worldviews.

As far back as 2500 B.C. there were three cradles of emerging *materia medica*. First was the island of Cos, the birthplace of Hippocrates, who developed the Hippocratic tradition of medicine that spread from Greece to Egypt, then to Persia in the east and on to Italy in the west. Second was the Yellow River area of China, where traditional Chinese medicine evolved. Third was the Indus Valley of India, the seat of Ayurvedic medicine.[227]

These three branches of ancient traditional medicine, though all different, were yet the same in many ways, mainly because of their cross-pollination by travelers and merchants. Some of the belief systems shared were "the separable soul, forerunner of vital essence," "elements as impersonal forces in nature" (pantheism), "the colon as the root of disease," "self-responsibility," "the role of karma and no concept of sin," "transmigration of the soul and reincarnation,"[228] and "diagnosis of the whole from the part (e.g., pulse diagnosis)."[229] Incidentally, pulse diagnosis is employed by the exiled Tibetan Buddhist leader and physician, the Dahli Lama.[230]

By the sixth century B.C., "the idea of wind as life force was developed in both Vedic and Iranian thought." By the same period, the Chinese "had absorbed the Babylonian astrological idea into its six-fold categories of yin and yang."[231]

Traditional Chinese Medicine (TCM)

"Chinese medicine is the child of Chinese religion,"[232] and at their core lies the same fundamental belief in the dual universal energy of chi and the five elements.[233]

Traditional Chinese medicine (TCM) is embodied in a written work of ideas and theories about disease and its treatments that are practiced by medical Chinese and other practitioner specialists. Chinese folk medicine, in contrast to TCM, is mainly empirical (based on practical experience), consisting of simple remedies used by non-professionals and informally educated practitioners.

TCM is extremely complex and intricate, involving acupuncture, acupressure, moxibustion, herbalism, diet, tai chi (body-mind exercise for energy balancing), Eastern meditation (altered states of consciousness), and yoga (disciplines).

Acupuncture, which employs the insertion of fine needles into various parts of the body, has been used and practiced by tens of millions in China and millions more around the world. Acupuncture's roots date back 2,500 years to the writings of Huang Di Nei Jing's *Yellow Emperor's Classic of Internal Medicine*.[234] This work, believed to be the oldest and most comprehensive medical classic in the world, is the basis of all Chinese medicine.[235]

The accumulation of all the previous philosophical concepts and practical experiences of yin-yang and the five elements were summed up into a unique system of medical theories in this third century BC canon of medicine.[236] The theories of yin-yang and visceral (internal) organs and meridians have since become the foundation of Chinese medicine.[237]

In the nineteenth century, European medicine reached the orient. Unrefined as European medicine was at the time, the Great Imperial Medical Board in 1822 ordered that acupuncture, which had been developed to the level of a pseudoscience, be abandoned in favor of Western medicine. Again in 1929, the same order was given by the Kuomintang government. But the practice of TCM, especially acupuncture, continued, mainly because there were not enough Western trained physicians to cover the vast population of China.[238]

When Communism took over in 1949, the Communist regime created a revival of TCM. Mao Tse-tung stressed the great heritage that the Chinese people had in their traditional medicine.[239]

Until 1971, very little was known about TCM in America. It was in that year that James Reston, an editorial columnist and vice president of *The New York Times*, traveled to China. While in Peking (Beijing), Reston suffered an attack of appendicitis. Following an operation, he suffered from gastritis (stomach cramps) and was successfully treated with acupuncture.

Upon his return to the United States, Reston wrote about his experience in *The New York Times* (22 August 1971), causing widespread interest. Within the following few months, journalists, scientists, and physicians traveled to China to observe acupuncture firsthand. Their observations were published in the American press and in some scientific journals.[240]

President Richard Nixon is credited with opening wide the doors for the influence of TCM in America when he visited Beijing in 1972. Nixon was seeking the normalization of relations between the United States and The People's Republic of China.

Acupuncture and the universal energy of chi/qi

Acupuncture is probably the best-known form of ancient traditional Chinese medicine and philosophy outside of China. It is widely practiced in Germany and the Scandinavian countries.

In spite of the comparatively low numbers of therapists in the U.S., acupuncture is one of the most visible alternate new age therapies. It has found adherents among American presidents (John F. Kennedy), movie stars (the late Lorne Greene), sports stars (Roman Gabriel), and among statesmen and royalty (Winston Churchill, Prince Bernard of the Netherlands).[241]

Acupuncture uses needles to allegedly stimulate the flow of chi/qi, which is the dual universal energy of yin and yang, in the body's 14 main invisible meridians (channels). These meridians correspond to the vital organs to regulate or restore (unclog) the balance of "universal energy" to relieve pain or cure illness.

> The theoretical basis of acupuncture and moxibustion is the theory of the meridians. According to this theory, there is a system of meridians (also called channels) in the body through which *qi* (vital energy) and blood circulate, and by which internal organs are coordinated and connected with superficial organs and tissues, creating an integral whole. There are certain points along the superficial part of the meridians reached by *qi* of the visceral organs. Acupuncturists use these points, called acupuncture points or acupoints; they are the places where the body surface is connected with the visceral organs. When one is ill, the flow of *qi* and blood can be regulated by stimulating certain points of the body surface through needling or moxibustion; illness of the associated internal organs can thus be cured.[242]

Moxibustion, mentioned in the above quotation, is used in conjunction with acupuncture for treatment of chronic pain. It is a method of applying heat to the acupoints to stimulate the flow of universal energy. The material used in moxibustion is "moxa-wool" in the form of a cone or stick. It is ignited and allowed to smolder, allowing heat to penetrate the surface of the skin at the acupoint.[243]

All traditional Chinese medicine is based on the Chinese Taoist philosophy of dual universal energy or life force called "chi" (also spelled "qi," or "ki"). Chi encompasses the two principles of yin and yang. This dual energy (yin and yang) supposedly permeates the universe and everything in the world, including humans. "Yin" is regarded as the negative force and "yang" as the positive force.

Chinese acupuncturists believe that pain and sickness are caused by blockage and congestion that prevents the balanced flow of yin and yang in the body. This condition can be alleviated, restoring health and relieving pain, by inserting fine needles at strategic acupoints. Some allege that there are one hundred fifty or even as many as two thousand acupoints[244] located on the twelve, or some say fourteen, invisible, vertical body channels, known as "meridians,"[245] the cardinal lines, and the "collaterals," the branches of this complex acupoint network, where yin and yang flow. According to the American Medical Association, the theory upon which acupuncture is based has not been proven either scientifically or physiologically.[246]

China Beijing International Acupuncture Training Center

In my search to understand the philosophy and the medical functions of acupuncture on the human body, I went to Beijing, Shanghai, and Hong Kong. I visited the prestigious China Beijing International Acupuncture Training Center to interview the Chinese authority on acupuncture at that center.

One morning I took a cab out to the International Acupuncture Center. I approached the receptionist with my request to see Cheng Xinnong, world-renowned acupuncturist professor. In her limited English, she told me that Professor Xinnong was very busy and besides, there was a three-month waiting list to see him. I told her that I had come all the way from America to interview him and would be leaving the next day and I needed to interview him. She said she was sorry but could not help me. I could not bear the thought that I would not get to interview this man for the project I was researching.

Then the Lord gave me an idea. Pulling out my business card, I showed it to the receptionist, pointed to my name, then to myself, and then pointed to my title: Vice President, North American Division of Seventh-day Adventists. She looked very carefully at the card, then at me, then at the card again. She then picked up the phone and talked to someone. In no time there was a young Chinese woman who appeared and was asked to take me to the acupuncturist professor for an interview where she would serve as the translator. I'm not sure what exactly made the difference, but I have a hunch that she probably saw "vice president" and "North America" and figured I was the vice president of the United States. A few minutes later I was ushered into the presence of the renowned professor. He was a small, thin, elderly gentleman dressed in a blue Mao suit, with long white hair, a Fu Manchu mustache and beard. I was able to interview him for forty minutes. During that time a group of doctors from Finland came by to meet him and were only allowed to come in the room, bow to him, and then were ushered on through the center. In the interview, I asked Professor Xinnong if he could identify the meridians in western medical, physiological or anatomical terms. He said No. He said they were mystical and there was no way of identifying them in western medical terms.

A couple of days earlier I had purchased some books on acupuncture, one of which was considered to be the best on the subject that had been translated into English. I asked Professor Xinnong if he would autograph it for me. Opening it to a blank page, I handed it to him. Through the interpreter, he told me "Not on that page." And he turned to the page where the chief editor's name was. To my surprise, he said, "That's my name. I'll sign it here." I have found that book to be a very good source of information about acupuncture. It states that the yin and yang concept is at the base of all Chinese medicine, which includes acupuncture: "The theory of yin and yang permeates all aspects of the theoretical system of traditional Chinese medicine. It serves to explain the organic structure, physiological functions and pathological changes of the human body, and in addition guides clinical diagnosis and treatment."[247]

Xie Zhu-Fan, M.D., in his book, *Best of Traditional Chinese Medicine*, very succinctly says the same thing: "The yin-yang philosophical concept of opposition predominates in traditional Chinese medicine."[248]

Professor Xinnong further states the Chinese belief that "qi" is the fundamental substance of the universe and the human body:

> According to ancient Chinese thought, qi was the fundamental substance constituting the universe, and all phenomena were produced by the changes and movement of qi. This viewpoint greatly influenced the theory of traditional Chinese medicine. Generally speaking, the word *qi* in traditional Chinese medicine denotes both the essential substances of the human body which maintain its vital activities, and the functional activities of the zang-fu organs and tissues.[249]

 Yin and yang—harmony of opposites philosophy
The yin and yang symbol, also known as the Tai chi symbol and as the Diagram of the Supreme Ultimate, is a circle composed of two matching black (yin)-and-white (yang) symbols in circular motion. This symbol stands for "the wholeness and infinity of Ki, having neither beginning nor ending, and pervading everything."[250]

The circular symbol of yin-yang is divided by a curved line denoting motion, change, and the constant flow of yin and yang.[251] These universal forces are bipolar, meaning that they are opposites, but complementary, not antagonistic. The two colors, black and white, are of equal proportion, creating a dynamic balance. "When there is more of one force, there is less of the other, and at their extremes they transform into each other."[252]

The Tai chi Taoist philosophy teaches that in order to have harmony in the universe and all that it encompasses, including the human body, there must be a balance of yin and yang, a negative and positive balance of the universal life force, as stated by Dr. Xie Zhu-Fan: "Although yin and yang are in opposition to each other, they are mutually dependent. Neither can exist in isolation."[253]

Even though the philosophy of yin and yang, the harmony of opposites, seems to make sense up to a certain point, it breaks down when, in order to have harmony, there needs to be a balance of good and evil. In the white portion (yang), there is a black dot, and in the black portion (yin), there is a white dot, denoting that there is nothing totally pure or perfect. More importantly, the dots signify that there are no "absolutes," meaning no right or wrong.

This symbol also teaches that males have a little element of feminism and vice versa. It is interesting to note that John the Revelator, the spirit entity that Kevin Ryerson sometimes channels, told Shirley MacLaine in a seance at her Malibu home, that figures such as Jesus and Buddha are "androgynous." In other words, they are highly spiritual individuals who know no sexual difference because both sexes are simultaneously present in them.

> Their yin and yang were so evenly distributed that sexuality was of no interest to them because there was no conflict and therefore no tension. It was not a subject they needed to sublimate or repress. It simply didn't interest them because of their peaceful spiritual level of achievement.[254]

At first glance, from a Westerner's perspective, the yin-yang symbol may appear to be very simple and insignificant, yet it represents a deep and universal theory of the universe and all that exists in it. For example, a Taoist can list everything in existence either under the yin or the yang. Under yin he lists night, moon, cold, left, negative, evil, weakness, and female. Under yang are the opposites of yin: day, sun, warmth, right, positive, goodness, strength, and male. Originally, the meaning of yin was "the shady side of the hill" and yang was the "sunny side of the hill."[255]

Even the vital organs are categorized as either yin or yang. For instance, the heart is yang and the kidneys are yin. This is important because categorizing vital organs works hand in hand with the theory of the Five Elements (fire, wood, water, metal, and earth) in diagnosing an illness and in determining treatment.

In traditional Chinese medicine, it is believed that the dual universal energy of chi moves throughout the body and flows specifically through invisible vertical pathways or channels of the body known as "meridians." When there is a balance between the yin (negative) and yang (positive) universal energies, there is health and vitality. When an imbalance of energy occurs or the flow of either of the universal forces is blocked or congested, pain or illness occurs.

Some Asian women hoard gold in their earlobes because of the yang (positive) quality of this precious metal, thereby compensating for their own yin (negative) qualities.

With yin and yang being the most important philosophy in traditional Chinese medicine (TCM), the basic tool for diagnosis and treatment is the theory of the Five Elements. Since the human body is believed to be a microcosm of the universe and the Five Elements determine the composition and the phenomena of the universe, these elements are used to diagnose the medical condition of a patient, as mentioned before. They are central to TCM:

> At the heart of traditional Chinese medicine is the Five Elements Theory, which healers use both to diagnose and treat illness. The Five Elements—Fire, Wood, Water, Metal, and Earth—link the seasons of the year, aspects of nature, the body's organs and specific foods, herbs and treatments. It is also used for agricultural planning, healing, psychology, maintaining harmony in relationships, and even divination. This incredible tool typifies the Chinese talent for seeing the unity within apparent diversity.[256]

Massage therapies—acupressure, shiatsu and reflexology

Another TCM method of healing using the acupoints is massage. In India and other countries of the Orient, touch is highly valued as a method of healing. Through touch, life energy is thought to be transmitted from one person to another. This is the basis for various types of massage therapy such as acupressure, shiatsu, and reflexology.[257] Acupressure is Chinese, shiatsu is Japanese, and reflexology is a Western variety of energy-balancing techniques. Though the massage techniques in the various therapies may vary, the idea that the therapy manipulates the flow of energy comes from the same source.

Acupressure is a finger massage based on the same principles and techniques as acupuncture except that instead of using needles, the treatment is done with finger pressure massaging over the acupoints.[258]

Shiatsu, which is a form of Japanese finger pressure massage, is also based on the universal energy known as "Ki" (the Japanese spelling of chi or qi) as in acupuncture and acupressure.[259]

Acupressure and shiatsu, just two of many Oriental disciplines, are massage techniques for transferring qi to specific acupuncture points and meridians. Rather than use needles, which *work as antennae to draw qi into the body* at specific points and along certain meridian lines, healing touch is used to stimulate qi and unblock meridians. This results in the reestablishment of the life force and the restoration of health (italics added).[260]

Attempts to define the flow of chi/qi

Most acupuncturists and acupressure enthusiasts are not overly concerned about isolating and identifying the meridians, collaterals, or acupuncture points in Western physiological medical terms. As long as it works, that is all that matters to them. No explanations are necessary.

However, a North Korean professor, Kim Bong Han, after extensive research on the subject, claimed that the acupuncture points and meridians correspond to ducts and superficial corpuscles in the skin.[261] A Russian surgeon, Mikhail Gaikin, and a physicist, Victor Adamenko, claim to have measured electrical resistance in the skin at precise points or at the acupuncture points.[262]

Felix Mann, in his book, *The Meridians of Acupuncture*, writes concerning qi that it "might" be "a wave of electrical depolarisation" moving in the meridians which are described as "a fibre of the autonomic nervous system." This reveals that even he is not sure what they really are or where they are, yet he is the president of The Medical Acupuncture Society in London.

This flow of essential energy, Qi, along the meridians *might* in reality be a wave of electrical depolarisation travelling along a fibre of the autonomic nervous system: the Qi being the electrical phenomenon, the meridian the fibre. (italics added).[263]

Dr. Peter Yuen, Director of the Loma Linda Center for Pain Management in Loma Linda, California, who by the way is a non-

Adventist alumnus of Loma Linda University, is the only doctor at the university who practices acupuncture. He uses it only for pain relief. In a telephone interview, I asked him if he could identify or isolate the meridians, collaterals, and acupoints in Western medical terms. His answer was, "No. It is very difficult. The only thing that comes close to identifying them is the Kirlian photography, which takes photographs of energy fields."[264]

Kirlian photography was invented in 1939 by S. D. Kirlian, a Russian electrician and amateur photographer. Using photographic plates to register invisible phenomena, he allegedly photographed the corona of an aura surrounding the human body. Auras, imperceptible to the physical sight, supposedly can be seen by clairvoyants. Clairvoyancy is believed to give the ability to perceive past, present, and future events, and the power to "see" disembodied spirits as in channeling and mediumship.[265]

Perhaps the best definition of the meridians and the collaterals is one that Will Baron (who has a certificate in acupressure) gave me during a personal interview. "They are," he said, "a mystical energy system that allegedly co-exists with the anatomical nervous system."[266]

The Chinese belief system encompasses monism and Confucianism, the moral teachings of Confucius. However, the average Chinese is hard-pressed to define monism, Taoism, and pantheism in their purest sense. Instead, his religious and philosophical beliefs include a combination of animism, Tao-Buddhism, folk myth, magic, fung shui (Chinese earth magic), ancestral worship, and the supernatural.[267] It is not surprising to discover that Taoist priests are often employed by modern developers of construction sites to deal with the spirits of the earth before breaking ground.

> Even the huge multi-million dollar Mass Transit Railway project, which gave Hong Kong the biggest modern underground railway in the world, started with an invocation given by a whole bank of Taoist priests. They paid respects to all the spirits of the earth who were about to be outraged by having their domain violated.[268]

Thus, both Chinese religion and culture, from which TCM received its existence, are integrally combined with occult spiritualistic elements which are also evident in their theories of wellness.

Universal healing energy, common denominator

It is interesting to note that the "universal healing energy" is a common denominator among many of the nonbiblical worldviews, although it bears different names in various cultures.

- In Taoism and ancient Chinese medicine, this dual universal healing energy is called *chi* (*qi*).
- In Japan, it is called *ki*.
- In Hinduism, it is referred to as *Prana*, "breath."
- In Greece, it is called *pneuma*.[269]
- The Polynesians refer to it as *Mana*.
- Native Americans call it *Orenda*.[270]
- Franz Anton Mesmer, father of modern hypnotism, referred to it as *animal magnetism*.[271]
- D. D. Palmer, founder of chiropractic, called it *The Innate*.[272]
- Wilhelm Reich, founder of Orgonomy, used the term *Orgone energy*.
- Samuel Hahnemann, founder of homeopathy, called it the *vital force*.[273]
- Baron Karl von Reichenback referred to it as the *Od force* or *Odyle*.[274]
- Contemporary Soviet parapsychologists call it *Bioplasma*.
- And George Lucas of *Star Wars* calls it *The Force*.[275]

We are told that, regardless of its name, this energy pervades everything in the universe, unites each individual to the cosmos, and is the doorway to untapped human potential. It is at the root of all healing, all psychic abilities, all so-called miraculous occurrences.[276]

Ellen White also used the term *vital force*. However, her use of *vital force* refers to the sum total of life expectancy that God has given each person. Our vital force can be lessened by sinful living and/or a violation of the natural laws of health. Ellen White mentions that "If Adam, at his creation, had not been endowed with twenty times as much vital force as men how have, the race, with their present habits of living in violation of natural law, would have become extinct."[277]

Applied kinesiology

Applied kinesiology is a unique blend of ancient Chinese medicine and American chiropractic theory that tests the muscles for organ dysfunction. Applied kinesiology is not to be confused with formal or standard kinesiology (biomechanics), a legitimate science, which is the study of bodily movements and the muscles that control them.

Dr. George Goodheart, a chiropractor and psychic, is considered the founder of applied kinesiology. In 1964 he was the first to teach that each large muscle relates to a body organ. When there is a weakness in a muscle, it is usually an indication that an energy problem exists in an associated organ. By treating the muscle to make it strong again, Goodheart was able to improve the functioning of the associated organ as well.[278]

Dr. Goodheart associated the standard kinesiology muscle-testing techniques with the Chinese universal energy chi that flows through the so-called meridians of the body. Dr. D. D. Palmer, founder of chiropractic, called this universal energy *innate* or *innate intelligence* that, he said, flows through the nervous system and is affected by the spinal cord.[279] The proponents of applied kinesiology allege that

> Every organ dysfunction is accompanied by a specific muscle weakness, which enables diseases to be diagnosed primarily through muscle-testing procedures. Its practitioners—most of whom are chiropractors—also claim that nutritional deficiencies, allergies, and other adverse reactions to food substances can be detected by placing substances in the mouth so that the patient salivates. "Good" substances will make specific muscles stronger, whereas "bad" substances will cause specific weaknesses.[280]

Applied kinesiology and behavioral kinesiology operate on the same principle of innate energy imbalance in the organs related to the muscle via the appropriate acupuncture meridians.[281]

The muscles are thought to be the energy pumps that increase the flow of innate energy through specific meridians. When the thymus gland is functioning properly, the flow of energy enhances wellness. When the thymus is not functioning correctly, the energy flow decreases, causing an imbalance that results in illness.[282] The thymus is believed to be the monitoring center for measuring the energy imbalances of the entire meridian system.[283]

The marked difference between applied kinesiology and behavioral kinesiology is that applied kinesiology tests the mechanical strength of the muscle while behavioral kinesiology tests the "the energy in the meridians associated with the muscles, and the ability of the body to replenish the energy."[284] Behavioral kinesiology also includes psychiatry and psychosomatic medicine.[285]

11

Ayurvedic Medicine, Eastern Meditation, and Other Occult Therapies

Ayurvedic medicine

Another ancient medical system that has greatly influenced the New Age holistic health movement is Ayurvedic medicine. Ayurvedic medicine, the traditional Hindu healing system, originated more than four thousand years ago.[286] *Ayurveda* comes from the Sanskrit words *ayur,* which means "life," and *veda,* which means "knowledge," and is based on the *Vedas,* the oldest known philosophical and sacred writings of the Hindus. Ayurvedic medicine is very much a part of Hindu spiritual life, for it was established by some of the same people who gave India its systems of meditation, yoga, and astrology.

> Ayurveda is a system of healing which evolved on the Indian subcontinent some 3000–5000 years ago. It was established by the same great ancient sages who produced India's original systems of meditation, yoga and astrology. Ayurveda has both a spiritual and a practical basis, the spiritual perspective engendering the practical.[287]

According to ayurvedic beliefs, humans consist of three aspects: the physical (body), the subtle (mind), and the causal (spirit). The harmonious function of all three parts of this trinity produces health.[288]

Like the Chinese Taoist and Greek Hippocratic systems,

Ayurvedic medicine sees health within a context of the universe based on a nonbiblical worldview. The Hindus believe that human life is an extension of the "cosmic consciousness" and that one's well-being depends on his relationship with the cosmic consciousness.[289] In ayurvedic medicine, the "marma points" are the equivalent to the acupoints of yin and yang energy. The "marma points" in Hindu medicine are the anatomical regions of the body through which "prana" (the same as qi) flows to maintain health.[290]

Like traditional Chinese medicine, ayurvedic medicine is a highly complex system of healing. It involves such practices as mind-body healing (healing is provided for both mind and body), aromatherapy, herbalism, biofeedback, yoga, meditation, macrobiotics, and energy manipulation. No attempt will be made to exhaust the teachings of Hindu ayurvedic medicine, only a focus on the basic philosophies, tracing the ayurvedic roots of yoga, biofeedback, and therapeutic touch.

A decade ago, Westerners knew very little about ayurvedic medicine. One of the persons most responsible for popularizing ayurvedic medicine in America is Dr. Deepak Chopra, a respected endocrinologist and the executive director of the Sharp Health Care Institute for Human Potential and Mind/Body Medicine in San Diego, California. Chopra was born and raised in New Delhi, India, and attended the All India Institute of Medical Sciences. He has written numerous books on health-related topics. In his book, *Quantum Healing: Exploring the Frontiers of Mind/Body Medicine*, which was highly endorsed by Marilyn Ferguson, New Age spokesperson and author of *The Aquarian Conspiracy*, Chopra combines ancient alternative medicine with Western medicine.

Time magazine called Chopra the "Emperor of the Soul" because of his combining medical advice with Indian metaphysics, "telling Americans where spirit and body interact." The article praised Chopra by saying: "The realm of New Age healing is composed of roughly four categories. Chopra's strength is that he is a combination of them all: an endocrinologist; a synthesizer of Indian medicine and quantum physics; a writer of great passion; and a propagator of magic and mysticism."[291]

Chopra is a Hindu mystic who embraces the monistic worldview concept that "on a cosmic level, we all exist simultaneously throughout the universe."[292] It is not difficult to see where Dr. Chopra is coming from and how he fits into the New Age alternative medicine movement.

Ayurvedic medicine is based on the Hindu belief that every person is made up of varying amounts of air, water, fire, earth, and ether, the Five Elements of creation. Ayurveda teaches that illness is a result of an imbalance of these elements, and that health can be obtained only by the restoration of their balance.[293] The Five Elements are housed in what are called the three metabolic body types (*doshas*), *vata, pitta,* and *kapha,* which are similar to the Western body types "thin," "muscular," and "fat." In Western medicine, such body types do not usually play a prominent part in diagnosis and treatment. However, in ayurvedic medicine, *doshas* are far more complex than just the body types per se and are regarded as having a much greater influence on a person's well-being than in Western medicine. *Doshas* pertain to the innate constitution of a person's body, moods, personality, and other characteristics. Within the *doshas* are the Five Elements.[294]

According to Dr. Chopra,

> When the *doshas* are balanced in accordance with an individual's constitution, the result is vibrant health and energy. But when the delicate balance is disturbed, the body becomes susceptible to outside stressors, which may range from viruses and bacteria to poor nutrition and overwork. Imbalance in the *doshas* is the first sign that mind and body are not perfectly coordinated.[295]

The basis of all treatments in the ayurvedic system is the balancing of the life energies within us. The life energies are collectively called "prana," which is the same as the Chinese chi or qi. "These forces were called yin and yang by the ancient Chinese sages and *rajas* and *tamas* by the Hindu seers, who also describe a third balancing force, *sattwa.*"[296]

Ayurvedic physicians, *vaidyas,* employ meditation as a primary and fundamental tool as well as "diet, herbs, mineral substances and aromas."[297] *Vaidyas* are also familiar with the principles of nutrition, psychology, astrology, gem and color therapy, herbal preparations, and climatology.

Those who are acquainted with the alternative New Age holistic health therapies will recognize that many of the above-mentioned therapies and practices definitely have their roots in ayurvedic medicine. Any therapy that utilizes energy balancing, manipulation of "prana" energy, altered states of consciousness, and aura readings can be traced to ayurvedic medicine. And ayurvedic medicine, like traditional Chinese medicine, is an oriental healing system based on a nonbiblical worldview and mystical forms of healing that cannot be supported by the Bible or the Spirit of Prophecy. In the book *Evangelism*, by Ellen White, a whole chapter (chapter 18) deals with the false healing practices of Christian Science, the occult, and Oriental religions. She warns against them because of the spiritual dangers, attributing their healing power to Satan and his demons.

Eastern mystical meditation

Eastern meditation, unlike biblical meditation, leads to "altered states of consciousness." It is a form of self-hypnosis, which can be spiritually detrimental. Altered states of consciousness, either self-induced (self- or auto-hypnosis, trance) or assisted by someone else using guided imagery, etc., can be spiritually dangerous because, in this condition, the person is rendered no longer in control and becomes open not only to the hypnotic suggestions of someone but also to demonic influence.

Eastern meditation plays a vital role in almost all of the New Age holistic therapies that derive from Hinduism, Buddhism, and Taoism. It is a tool used to aid the patient in connecting with "ultimate reality," for healing or effecting his own body's recovery to wellness by the process of visioning his internal organs, as done in hatha yoga, biofeedback, and a number of other New Age holistic health therapies. Therefore, in the New Age holistic health movement, Eastern mystical meditation and holistic health therapies work hand in hand.

Dr. Deepak Chopra states that "those who attain some harmony with that universal mind by meditating and following Ayurvedic practices could avoid various diseases."[298]

New Age holistic medicine, which has borrowed many of its techniques from traditional Chinese medicine and ayurvedic medicine, employs, to a great extent, mystical meditation. Transcendental Meditation (a watered-down version of Hindu mystical meditation) is also employed by New Age practitioners as a tool to help patients back to health. In *Alternative Medicine: The Definitive Guide*, it is stated that

> Studies have also shown that meditation, [in particular, research on Transcendental Meditation (TM), a popular form of meditation practiced in the West for the past thirty years] can bring about a healthy state of relaxation by causing a generalized reduction in multiple physiological and biochemical markers, such as decreased heart rate, decreased respiration rate, decreased plasma cortisol (a major stress hormone), decreased pulse rate, and increased EEG (electro-encephalogram) alpha, a brain wave associated with relaxation.[299]

This complete volume on alternative medicine, in the same chapter, entitled "Meditation," recommends meditation as "well-suited to self-care" and adds that it "can become part of your personal health maintenance program."[300] Eastern meditation or any kind of meditation that involves forms of self-hypnosis and visioning is occultic, mystical, and spiritually dangerous.

Yoga

Hinduism teaches its followers to seek for spiritual enlightenment within themselves and for ultimate release, *moksha*, from rebirth and the phenomenal world. The yogas are metaphysical pathways or metaphysical spiritual disciplines to assist in attaining release and liberation from the outside world and to unite with "ultimate reality." This type of metaphysical spiritual discipline requires asanas (proper postures such as the lotus position), rhythmic breathing, intense concentration and focusing, introspective meditation, and the repetition of the proper thought formulas as Aum, Om.[301]

The word *yoga* is a Sanskrit word literally meaning "to unite." The closest English word is *yoke*. Yoga implies uniting oneself to ultimate reality. In Hinduism, "ultimate reality" can be the true self, an impersonal absolute and/or a personal deity such as Brahma or Krishna.[302] Yoga ascetic spiritual disciplines can be considered Hindu-styled forms of Christian meditation and prayer. There are many yogas. However, the seven main ones are:

(1) hatha yoga—controlling the physical body through postures, pranayama, and "purification" practices (kriyas)

(2) laya yoga—kundalini, the chakras, and bodily sounds audible when the ears are covered

(3) mantra (or nada) yoga—mind control

(4) jnana (or nana) yoga—understanding the laws of the universe

(5) bhakti yoga—devotion to a god

(6) karma yoga—selfless service, duty, and behavior control; and

(7) raja (ashtanga or astanga) yoga, which encompasses all the foregoing schools.[303]

Yoga was introduced to America in 1890 when the Theosophical Society published the first book that explained and advocated the practice, *Nature's Finest Forces*, by Rama Prasad. The Theosophical Society subsequently became the "major conduit of Eastern teachings to Westerners, and along with the full range of Hindu and Buddhist thought, the society supplied materials on yoga."[304]

Once yoga had been introduced, yoga teachers immigrated to America to teach it during the early decades of the twentieth century. B.K.S. Iyengar's book, *Light on Yoga*, "the most comprehensive volume on hatha yoga ever produced," became the most popular book on yoga technique and instruction in America. In the 1970s, bhakti yoga became very popular through the Hare Krishna movement.[305]

The best-known form of yoga in America today is hatha yoga, the yoga discipline that teaches control of the physical body through posture as asana, proper yoga position. The most recognized posture of hatha yoga is the familiar cross-legged sitting position called "lotus." The handstand is another hatha yoga asana.

YMCAs, YWCAs, colleges, and physical fitness centers offer hatha yoga as a physical mind exercise to reduce stress. Though hatha yoga can reduce stress levels, its purpose is far beyond mere stress reduction. It is a means of acquiring, through the practice of strict breath control, meditation, visualization, and the incorporation of asanas, the ability to control the normally uncontrollable physiological functions of the body (breathing, blood flow, metabolism, etc.). The breathing techniques awaken the different levels of consciousness, of which there are six, and illuminate the soul. "Thus, breath is regarded as more than a gateway to the inner being; it is a door to the divine within each of us. In the East, the science of breath is ultimately a religious path."[306] And that religious path is none other than Hinduism!

In India, it is not the young collegiates who practice hatha yoga. It is rather the elderly who do it. In the last few years of their lives, devoted Hindus practice hatha yoga, learning how to control those bodily functions that are normally not consciously controllable, to the point of eventually being able to turn them off at will. This art is learned in preparation for their own death, by their consciously turning off all bodily functions, and entering into the next life by reincarnation.[307]

In his book, *The Other Side of Silence: A Guide to Christian Meditation*, Morton T. Kelsey, Catholic priest and a well-known New Age author, describes the inherent danger of imaging in an altered state of consciousness because the individual no longer has conscious control. His book title is somewhat of a misnomer, because the so-called "Christian" meditation he describes is a carbon copy of Eastern mystical meditation.

It is true that imagination requires a very different capacity. With imagination one does not have conscious control of the images worked with. They cannot be called up or stopped at will like concepts can. Images are more like living beings with a life and purpose of their own. Often they take the individual into strange territory where he or she does not know the terrain well enough to take direction and has trouble enough simply trying to follow where the images lead.[308]

Kelsey gives further warnings concerning meditation.

> Meditation is not something one should do simply because others are doing it. It cannot be undertaken like an aesthetic exercise or merely for diversion. Whether we expect it or not, in meditation we are opening the door to another aspect of reality, potentially just as rewarding and sometimes even more dangerous than the physical world. . . . In addition, there is a reality of radical evil found in the inner world that is bent on seizing power and destroying the individual.[309]

Those who practice laya yoga, whose object is to awaken the kundalini or "coiled snake" power at the base of the spine, can end up in madness, if the awakening occurs all of a sudden. Says Gopi Krishna, author of *Living with Kundalini*,

> In the case of those in whom the awakening occurs all at once as the result of yoga or other spiritual practices, the sudden impact of powerful vital currents on the brain and other organs is often attended with grave risk and strange mental conditions, varying from moment to moment, exhibiting in the beginning the abnormal peculiarities of a medium, mystic, genius, and madman all rolled into one.[310]

Christian writers John Ankerberg and John Weldon also warn that

> Although the public falsely perceives yoga as a safe or neutral practice, even authoritative yoga literature is replete with warnings of serious physical consequences, mental derangement, and harmful spiritual effects. Paralysis, insanity, and death are frequently mentioned. Allegedly, such consequences arise from wrong yoga practice, but, in fact, they really arise because yoga is an occult practice. Those who care about their overall health should not practice yoga.[311]

All yogas, whether they be hatha, karma, or bhakti, are Hindu, metaphysical spiritual pathways that lead to altered states of consciousness, self-awareness, and higher consciousness, eventually connecting the individual to supernatural powers. All of these mystical experiences are occultic in nature and therefore should not be a part of the Christian's lifestyle.

Biofeedback

Biofeedback has been referred to as the "electronic yoga" of the West, because through electronic devices it can teach the patient essentially the same thing that hatha yoga does—conscious control of the inner bodily workings or of the normally involuntary bodily functions and their physical responses.

C. Norman Shealy, M.D., Ph.D., who was the first president of the American Holistic Medical Association, associates biofeedback with occult medicine.

> I think occult medicine is the most dramatic, exciting, and provocative aspect of medical care today, the one with the greatest potentiality—if only because it's the least developed and explored. It includes such seemingly strange approaches as teaching people to control their own inner bodily workings just as the yogis of the East do—to slow the heart rate or lower the blood pressure, even to control epileptic seizures. This is the approach of biofeedback and autogenic training, twin manifestations of the same process.[312]

He further states that

> The achievements of yoga point us toward biofeedback and autogenics, the mechanical and the verbal aspects of the same phenomenon. Where biofeedback uses modern electronics, autogenics uses the simple basics of language and thought to achieve the same end, the control of body processes. Along with transcendental meditation, Zen, yoga, and other meditative disciplines, they work by some mechanism which is still not understood.[313]

Through the use of special electronic monitoring devices, such as electro-myograms (EMG), to observe muscle tension, electro-encephalograms (EEG), to monitor brain wave activity, and mental exercises (meditation and visualization), biofeedback attempts to train a person to consciously control blood flow, metabolism, skin temperature, breathing, heartbeat, and other involuntary bodily functions. The EEG machine acts as a mind mirror that measures and gives readings (feedback) on the brain-wave activities.

According to biofeedback practitioners, there are basically four brain waves: (1) beta waves, that "signify that the brain is in a state of normal waking awareness, (2) alpha waves, which "seem to be present during all the higher levels of awareness and when the mind is very calm and the body is relaxed," (3) theta waves, that "occur during meditation and at times of creative inspiration," and (4) delta waves, which "signify the rhythm of sleep, but also occur in waking people in response to new ideas, and in healers and psychics."[314]

It is noteworthy that "modern New Age brain-stimulation equipment has been compared to that of Buddhist or Hindu mandalas"[315]—circular designs that contain concentric geometric forms, images of deities, etc., symbolizing the universe, totality, wholeness, and oneness.[316]

Biofeedback, operating on the same principles as hatha yoga, definitely has its roots in Hinduism. Some extreme examples of mind-over-matter control are mentioned in Marvin Karlins' and Lewis M. Andrews' book, *Biofeedback: Turning on the Power of Your Mind*. A frail, scantily dressed 48-year-old yogi by the name of Shri S. R. Khrishna Iyengar volunteered at the All-India Institute of Mental Health in Bangalor, India, to be used as an experiment to test the breathing control of a yogi. He was put into a pit excavated to rigid specifications by the hospital staff. The yogi was wired up with an electrical instrument so that his vital functions could be monitored, laid on his back, and buried alive in the pit with a wooden plank over him, allowing him only a cubic meter of air to breathe. To make the situation even more challenging, the yogi lit an incense stick and put it at his side. In order to survive, the yogi had to reduce his metabolism enough to sustain himself with the minimal air seepage that came through the dirt—and he did so for nine hours.[317] In India, yogis teach themselves to control their bodily functions as yogi Shri did. In America, to achieve the same control, EEG machines are employed.

For the Christian, the danger in biofeedback does not lie with the use of electronic monitoring devices but with its use of Eastern meditative visualization techniques in altered states of consciousness.

Aromatherapy

A holistic health therapy that is winning converts, especially among women, is aromatherapy. Body Shops all over the country, through their cosmetic products, are promoting this ancient mind-body therapy that purports to heal with oils of flowers, plants, and herbs. Aromatherapy is

> the therapeutic use of the essential oils of plants. These oils are said to be very concentrated substances extracted from flowers, leaves, stalks, fruits, and roots, and also distilled from resins. They are said to represent the "life force" or "soul" of the plant. The oils are administered in small quantities through massage, or inhalation, or through creams and lotions. Occasionally, a product is taken internally.[318]

A trained aromatherapist is said to be able to decide which oils are best suited to a person's condition and "applies them to the specific energy points of the face and body. Here touch is as important as smell."[319]

Some aromatherapists can determine what oil or oils should be used by examining a lock of hair or a sample of handwriting from the patient, testing it in a dowsing ritual. The American Medical Association's *Reader's Guide to Alternative Health Methods* states that "there is no scientific evidence that the benefits achieved by aromatherapy are greater than those achieved by the power of suggestion."[320]

Even though very little physical harm may be done with these colognes, shampoos, and body oils, and certain aromas may indeed help a person to relax, anyone getting involved with aromatherapy should be aware that the practitioners may be involved with the New Age, occult ideas, and should exercise due caution.

Other Occult Therapies

Homeopathy

One of the most "apparently innocent" forms of New Age alternative medicine is homeopathy, based on the Law of Similars, that "like cures like." The word itself comes from two Greek words, *homoiois*, meaning "like," and *pathos* meaning "pain" or "suffering." Samuel Hahnemann, a German physician in the late eighteenth century, is largely credited with the development of this form of medicine. Homeopathy, like acupuncture, is based on the Chinese theory of universal energy, chi, which has yet to be scientifically isolated, observed, or measured.[321]

Hahnemann taught four basic principles regarding homeopathy:

1. A substance which produces symptoms in a healthy person cures those symptoms in a sick person.

2. The dynamic vital force is primarily affected in an individual who is sick, and therefore the medicine itself must be able to affect this by being itself dynamic.

3. The patient needs only one particular medicine at a time.

4. The totality of symptoms is what must be prescribed on, or a remedy found for.[322]

"Not even one molecule left"

Homeopathic remedies are prepared by using minerals, botanical substances, zoological substances, and other sources, weakened by multiple dilutions. Homeopathic Dr. George Vithoulkas states that

> Modern homeopaths use potencies up to the hundred thousandth centesimal and beyond. . . . The implications of this discovery are staggering. A substance shaken and diluted to a dilution of 1 in 100,000 parts, even to a total of 60 zeros and more, still acts to cure disease, quickly and permanently, and without side effects![323]

Dr. Vithoulkas goes on to say that "clearly this phenomenon cannot be explained by ordinary chemical mechanisms. The dilutions are so astronomical that *not even one molecule of the original medicine is left*."[324]

So if not even one molecule of the original medicine is left, what is it that cures the patients? According to the founder, it is the "spirit-like essence."

> Hahnemann himself believed that there is virtually no chance that even one molecule of original substance would remain after extreme dilutions. But he said that the vigorous shaking or pulverizing with each step of dilution leaves behind *a spirit-like essence* which cures by reviving the body's "vital force" (italics added).[325]

Astronomical dilutions that are said to contain not even one molecule of the original substance have to be the most incredible placebo to cure illnesses in modern times. Use of them is comparable to treating one's malaria by emptying an eight-ounce bottle of quinine into the Pacific Ocean off the shores of Japan while a typhoon is raging and then taking a spoonful from the ocean off the Malibu coast of Southern California and believing that it contains the essence of the spirit of the original quinine.

Some people think that homeopathic medicine is based on the same principle as vaccinations. With vaccines, a very small quantity of a virus is injected into an individual to force the immune system to produce antibodies against it. But homeopathy works on a different principle. Vaccines are given to build antibodies to protect healthy people from getting a disease, whereas homeopathy treats a sick patient with the essence or spirit of a substance that produces the same symptoms as his or her disease in a healthy person. Homeopathic treatments have nothing to do with the immune system and everything to do with restoring "vital force," or "dynamis" as Hahnemann called it.[326]

Hahnemann believed that

> True disease was not a physical entity. Rather, illness began at the spiritual level as an aberration or imbalance of the spirit-like power, or the vital principle that animates the human body. Only later does this aberration manifest as physical illness or disease. . . . Because the

true cause of disease is "spiritual," it must be treated with a "spiritual" medicine or remedy.[327]

Homeopathic remedies are described as "natural" and sold in health food stores. But in most cases, the homeopathic remedies contain only an "essence" or the "spirit" of the original substance, making it more spiritualistic than natural, not to mention that homeopathy is also based on a non-biblical worldview similar to the worldview of Taoists and Hindus, which includes the philosophies of pantheism and animism.

Therapeutic touch

Energy manipulation in its broadest sense includes acupuncture and acupressure, Shiatsu, applied kinesiology, aromatherapy, crystal energy balancing, reflexology, and Reiki (the laying on of hands to apply the universal energy "Ki" to promote healing and wellness). An additional energy manipulation therapy that is now widely practiced and promoted by the nursing profession is therapeutic touch.

Dolores Krieger, R.N., Ph.D., the founder and one of the chief promoters of therapeutic touch, was greatly influenced by the healing theories and practices of Ayurvedic, Tibetan, Chinese, and Native American medicine and yoga in resurrecting the ancient healing art of the therapeutic use of hands.[328] Therapeutic touch (TT) is considered to be America's equivalent of Reiki. Reiki is an energy healing system very similar to therapeutic touch based on ancient Tibetan medicine.[329]

The main principle of therapeutic touch is that the body is nurtured and maintained by prana, a vital energy force. Healthy people are believed to have an over-abundance of prana, whereas ill people have a deficiency. Essentially, the treatment consists of a therapist's extending his or her hands slightly above the patient's body, locating excess-energy fields and moving energy to deficient areas in the body where it is needed. At no time is there physical contact between the patient and the therapist.[330]

When introducing the four phases of therapeutic touch, Dolores Krieger called it "a healing meditation."[331] The four phases are as follows:

1. "Centering oneself physically and psychologically."[332] This first step is important because the TT practitioner must get into an intuitive state of consciousness.

2. "Exercising the natural sensitivity of the hand to assess the energy field of the healee for cues to differences in the quality of energy flow."[333] This second step is also called "assessment." The healer places his or her hands, face down, two to four inches above the patient and slowly scans the patient's energy field until a tingling or pulsation is felt in the hands of the healer.

3. "Mobilizing areas in the healee's energy field that the healer may perceive as being non-flowing; that is, sluggish, congested, or static."[334] Step 3 is very similar to the unclogging of chi in acupuncture to allow the balanced flow of yin and yang. In this moving phase, the hands become more active and the healer may engage in sweeping motions along the patient's body. The healer then vigorously shakes his or her hands to get rid of unwanted, excess negative energy.

4. "The conscious direction by the healer of his or her excess body energies to assist the healee to repattern his or her own energies."[335] The fourth step is transferring one's own vital energy to a patient, acting as a conduit of "healing universal energy" until the patient's energy fields are stabilized. In Krieger's words,

> During therapeutic touch, the person playing the role of healer literally becomes a human support system, supplementing the energies in [the patient's] own behalf. This dynamic human field interaction can reach very deeply within the psyche of both healer and healee.[336]

In ayurvedic medicine there are perceived to be seven chakras or main energy centers in the human body, recognized as agents for storing universal energy. Krieger states that the center depression in the palms is a secondary chakra energy center. That is the reason why the extended hands are used with palms down for therapeutic healing. Krieger has no apologies for adopting the traditional Chinese concept of maintaining an energy balance of yin and yang in the body, as well as the Ayurvedic concept of energy balancing of "prana."

Some Christians in America are very concerned about this controversial therapeutic touch method that is making inroads into the

Christian community. *Christianity Today* reports that to date upwards of "100,000 American nurses have been trained in therapeutic touch" and adds that it is one of the fastest-growing alternative-nursing practices, mainly because it is "non-invasive, nontoxic, and useful for pain reduction and the promotion of health."[337]

The Health Robbers: A Close Look at Quackery in America, edited by Stephen Barrett, M.D., and William T. Jarvis, Ph.D., president of the National Council against Health Fraud, headquartered in Loma Linda, California, states that there is no scientific evidence for the claims of therapeutic touch, and no studies validating TT have ever been reported in a reputable scientific journal.[338] It is obvious to those who have investigated therapeutic touch that it is based on an occultic form of energy manipulation.

Iridology

Like other New Age holistic health therapies, iridology is based on the perception of mystical universal energy fields in the body. This diagnostic method, examining the iris of the human eye for indications of illness, can be traced back to the ancient Chinese and Japanese, who are said to have been the first to peer into the iris to diagnose illnesses. The Babylonian Chaldeans and the Egyptians both suggested that the human eye played a significant role in medicine.[339]

In the nineteenth century, Ignatz von Peczely, an eleven-year-old Hungarian boy, accidentally broke the leg of his pet owl. Immediately, young Peczely observed a black stripe rising in the owl's eye. When he later became a physician, he recalled the incident and began studying the eyes of his patients.[340] It was in the early 1800s that he developed the first chart on iridology.

It was Dr. Bernard Jensen, however, who is considered the father of iridology. Jensen pioneered iridology in America and further developed von Peczely's chart of iridology to what it is today. Dr. Jensen's chart, which resembles Hindu teachings, outlines ninety-six zones or divisions of the eye just as the Hindus divided the "third-eye chakra." This inner-eye chakra, which is supposedly located on the forehead between the eyes, has a corresponding foot massage point located in "the area of the sinus at the tip of the big toe." In fact, all the seven Hindu chakras are said to be affected by massaging their corresponding massage points on the foot, just as in reflexology. The inner-eye chakra is not connected to any organ or part of the body but is believed to be universal, affecting the organism as a whole.[341]

According to iridologists, the iris serves as a map of the body and in some detail gives the health status of every organ system in the body. The indicators in the iris show up as dark lines, spots, or various color shades and patterns that serve as "warning signs for physical, mental and spiritual problems."[342]

Reader's Guide to Alternative Health Methods, published by the American Medical Association, condemns iridology on the basis that it is not scientific. Steve Barrett and William Jarvis in their book *The Health Robbers* state that in 1979

> Jensen and two other iridologists flunked a scientific test in which they examined photographs of the eyes of 143 persons in an attempt to determine which ones had kidney disease. (Forty-eight had been medically diagnosed as impaired using creatinine clearance tests, while the rest had normal kidney function.) The iridologists scored no better than chance.[343]

It is true that the iris of the eye is connected to the nervous system, but as Dr. Warren Peters, Director of the Center for Health Promotion at Loma Linda University states, "It is hardly the nerve center of the whole body."[344] Conventional medical doctors examine the pupil of the eye and check the sclera or "white of the eye" for unnatural brightness or yellowness which result from conditions such as atherosclerosis, diabetes, tuberculosis, and syphilis. However, conventional doctors do not recognize the connection of the iris to the vital parts of the body as detailed in Dr. Jensen's iridology chart.

Iridology shares many of the mystical concepts of the Hindu chakra energy fields, which puts it in the category of questionable occult holistic health practices. Most practitioners of iridology are chiropractors and naturopaths who, along with lay persons who do "nutrition" counseling, are also considered to be part of the New Age holistic health movement.

Reflexology

Reflexology, also known as "hand reflexology," "foot reflexology," and "zone therapy," is a form of massage on the sole of the foot or the palm of the hand. Reflexologists believe that the bottom of the foot and the inside of the hand contain nerve endings connecting the vital organs with other specific parts of the body. They believe that by pressure massaging and stroking specific areas of the hands and feet, they can affect these areas in the body. One of the purposes of reflexology is to balance perfectly the corresponding body functions. The saying among some reflexologists is, "When one holds a person's feet in one's hand, one has hold of his soul."[345]

Reflexology is related to the New Age holistic health energy-manipulating therapies, such as acupuncture, acupressure, applied kinesiology, Reiki, and therapeutic touch. Reflexology is considered a "novel" form of acupressure because, like acupuncture, it manipulates and attempts to balance the life energy force of chi.[346]

Dr. William Fitzgerald is the physician credited with rediscovering reflexology, which has its roots in ancient Chinese acupressure. In 1913, Dr. Fitzgerald introduced and developed the reflexology of modern times. He divided the area on the bottom of each foot into five zones corresponding to ten areas in the body. The ten zones ran from the tip of the ten fingers up to the arms and the neck, to the top of the skull, and then downward through the body to the legs, finally culminating in the ten toes. The zones originating in the left hand covered the left side of the body and those in the right hand covered the right side.[347]

Some reflexologists believe that 72,000 nerve endings at the bottom of the feet are connected to different body parts. By massaging these nerve endings, the corresponding body parts are affected. Other reflexologists say it is not the nerve endings that are massaged, but the chi dual energy of yin and yang along the meridian acupressure points.

The theory on which reflexology is based is that the human body works as a unit or a whole so that when one part is affected, the whole is affected. A healthy body is free from congestion, while a sick body is congested. Congestion, which interferes with the proper circulation of energy, is detected by the tender area or areas on the bottom of the foot. "This tenderness is caused by crystalline deposits which form at the nerve endings of the feet."[348] The deposits have to be either worked out or crushed to improve the circulation of the body. As Dr. Maybelle Segal states,

> The purpose in doing compression foot massage is to break up these deposits (or crush them) so that they may become solvent and be carried away with the rest of the waste material in the body. Once these deposits are dissolved, the congestion is relieved, and the circulation of the body is improved. Since the body works as a unit, the malfunctioning of even one part of the body will affect the rest of it.[349]

Theoretical physicist Fritjof Capra, author of *The Tao of Physics*, can help explain the reflexology treatment that applies therapy to a small part of the body and is able to affect the whole by borrowing a concept from quantum physics that states "that each component of a large entity may contain an image of the whole."[350]

The roots of reflexology are traceable back to ancient forms of pressure therapy known in Egypt as early as 3000 B. C.[351] It also has elements of the universal energy forces basic to traditional Chinese medicine and ayurvedic medicine, which makes it yet another entryway into the subtle New Age movement.

Pendulum divination

The use of a pendulum for divination purposes is a modern form of the ancient practice of divining, divination, or dowsing. Dowsing, which generally uses a "Y-rod" or "divining rod" made from a tree branch, was and continues to be used to identify and locate underground water, minerals, treasures, etc. In pendulum divination, the bob can be any object that will not conduct electricity, dangling from a string.[352] It goes beyond dowsing in that it claims to detect and measure energy fields, positive and negative, on both objects and individuals. Pendulum bobs can be as simple as a button or needle hanging on a string or as elaborate as gold or a semi-precious stone. Beginners are counseled to use material related to their sign of the Zodiac.[353]

Whereas dowsing detects things hidden from view, the pendulum method encompasses a far greater range of life awareness, divining in matters of everyday living, health-related problems, and spirituality. Basically, pendulums work on a premise of either placing the pendulum over an object or simply asking the pendulum questions that require a "yes" or "no" answer. If the pendulum rotates or swings clockwise, the answer s ignifies a positive, yes, male quality. If it swings counter-clockwise, in a circular fashion, it indicates a negative, no, or female quality answer.

In matters of diagnosing and prescribing remedies and therapies, the pendulum is suspended over the patient's organ or other area affected by disease, and the practitioner, called a "pendulumist," asks questions of the pendulum, such as: "Is this organ malfunctioning?" "Is the organ hyperactive?" "Is the organ inflamed?" Based on the pendulum's motion response, the machine is able to diagnose and recommend a therapy or remedy.

When the patient is not able to be present for any reason, a sketch of the body can be used and the same questions asked. Diagnosing from a distance is called "teleradiesthesia."

New Ager Greg Nielsen, author and authority on pendulum divination, associates pendulum divination with astrology, auras, spiritual frequencies, and New Age music. In his own words, he identifies the pendulum as a tool that will lead one into the New Age movement. "If you are a New Ager this book is a must. It not only takes you step by step to pendulum proficiency, but also specifically guides you into the New Age . . . the step in evolution: becoming an energy being."[354]

Even though the pendulum is used by some Christians, it should be pointed out that God specifically mentions "divination" in Deuteronomy 18:9-14 as an "abomination."

12

New Age Holistic Health Pioneers

Recent New Age holistic health pioneers

Although some New Age holistic medicine and therapies were developed within the past two hundred years, they were greatly influenced by ancient traditional Chinese medicine and Ayurvedic/Hindu medical philosophies. Many of these alternative medical treatments came out of an era when conventional medicine and science was at a low ebb. Treatments such as bleeding, leeching, and purging were among conventional treatments used at that time.

History records that the first president of the United States, George Washington, died partly as a result of his doctor repeatedly bleeding him during an illness. Such practices did little to enhance the credibility of contemporary medicine.

Thus the opportunity was open for the development of alternative forms of treatment that seemed better than the conventional treatments of the day. Very little, however, is ever mentioned by the New Agers about the personalities who developed their alternative medical treatments. When information is given, it is usually brief and the personalities are placed in a very positive light.

From the following sampling of recent New Age holistic health pioneers, we will discover some of their underlying beliefs and philosophies that coincide with New Age occult philosophy and thinking.

Samuel Hahnemann, father of homeopathy

Samuel Hahnemann (1755–1843) was a respected German physician who, in the eighteenth and early nineteenth centuries, was appalled at the dominant allopathic medical treatments of the day. He set out to develop the system of homeopathic medicine, which is based on the doctrine of similars or "Let like be cured by like."[355] Homeopathy is considered the epitome of New Age medicine because it adheres to occultic principles and practices. Hahnemann was an apparent spiritist and a follower of the famous spiritist and medium Emanuel Swedenborg. He was also a Freemason, which presented him with an excellent opportunity to delve into mysticism and the occult. Hahnemann was greatly influenced by animism and Eastern religion. "The reverence for Eastern thought was not just Hahnemann's personal hobby, but rather the fundamental philosophy behind the preparation of homeopathic remedies."[356]

It is obvious that Samuel Hahnemann was greatly influenced by the spiritualists of his day and developed a medical alternative that coincided with occult beliefs.

Mary Baker Eddy, founder of Christian Science and New Thought

Mary Baker Eddy founded one of the five largest denominations that emerged in America in the 1800s (1879), the Church of Christ, Scientist (Christian Science). One of the others was the Seventh-day Adventist Church. Eddy, at the age of 41, was crippled with a spinal problem that the conventional medicine of her day was unable to cure. So she went to a famous mind-body magnetic physician, Phineas Parkhurst Quimby, who treated and healed her with techniques based on Franz Anton Mesmer's primitive form of hypnotism, dubbed "mesmerism" along with his own technique of "gentle suggestions." This intrigued Mary Baker Eddy, who then developed her own metaphysical theory of healing, incorporating Quimby's and Mesmer's healing methods into her own Christian beliefs.

In 1875, Eddy published her theories in a book titled *Science and Healing with Keys to the Scriptures*. Its basic tenet stated that sickness is an illusion, that disease is linked to "errors" of the mortal mind, namely fear, ignorance, and sin. "According to her system, healing comes when the errors of the mortal mind are cast out by the giving of oneself to the divine mind or God."[357] Christian Scientists reject all conventional and orthodox medicine.

Even though the Church of Christ, Scientist was founded by Mary Baker Eddy, its metaphysical roots go back to Franz Anton Mesmer,[358] almost 100 years earlier, and his invisible, universal "magnetic fluid," dubbed "animal magnetism, which the Taoists call "chi" and the Hindus call "prana." This "universal energy" has never been identified or isolated scientifically.

A significant outgrowth of Christian Science is a philosophy called "New Thought," which helped pave the way for the New Age movement. Essentially, New Thought was articulated anew by Mary Baker Eddy's student, Emma Curtis Hopkins. It teaches that "mind, consciousness, ideas and thoughts are the basis of reality and the causal forces behind the material objects, events and conditions." That ultimate reality is the mind, that our life and our world are products of our thoughts.[359] In other words, New Thought teaches in part that one can create his own reality, which is part of New Age thinking.

Edgar Cayce—supernatural remedies

Edgar Cayce (1877–1945), called the "Sleeping Prophet," is considered one of the precursors to the New Age movement's holistic health component. Cayce was born on March 18, 1877, near Hopkinsville, Kentucky. His religious upbringing was in the Christian church (Disciples of Christ). He is best remembered as the last great traveling clairvoyant, who used his psychic powers to gain readings on health and recall the past lives of his patients. More than 30,000 of these psychic readings were recorded and are still referred to by those interested in this phenomenon.[360]

Though Cayce had a Christian background, he was greatly influenced by people who practiced parapsychology. In 1900, at the age of twenty-three, Cayce caught a cold that developed into laryngitis. An amateur hypnotist who knew Cayce put him into a trance, during which Cayce began to speak in a voice not his own. Speaking in the third person, he used the word *we* and began to prescribe a treatment for himself in great detail. Thus he was able to diagnose his own physical condition and prescribe his own cure. In 1909, Cayce met Dr. Wesley Ketchum, a homeopathic physician who requested that Cayce give him a reading. Dr. Ketchum was healed after following the advice Cayce gave him.

In 1923 Cayce met a wealthy printer, Arthur Lammers, who was a student of the occult and theosophy. Lammers introduced Cayce to the concept of reincarnation, which Cayce embraced. From that time forward, Cayce added past-life readings to the readings he gave people. In 1931 Cayce, along with his family and supporters, like Drs. William and Gladys McGarey, co-founded the Association for Research and Enlightenment (A.R.E.), famous for Cayce's nocturnal, psychic, spirit-channeled medical remedies, which resulted in thousands of pages addressing health issues. Although he was the key figure in this clinic, he himself admitted that "I've never studied physiology, or biology, or chemistry or anatomy."[361] His psychic alternative method of diagnosing and prescribing treatments was totally based on the occultic practice of channeling spirit entities.

Bernard Jensen—U.S. father of iridology

Although iridology was developed by Ignatz von Peczely and Neils Liljeuist, Bernard Jensen was considered the "U.S. father" of iridology. Jensen, a naturopathic physician and holistic health advocate, spearheaded the renewed popularity of this diagnostic tool in the New Age movement through his writings and lectures. His New Age philosophies are evident in his extensive bibliographies, which list New Age authors and their books, like H. P. Blavatsky's *Isis Unveiled*; Marilyn Ferguson's New Age handbook, *Aquarian Conspiracy*; parapsychologist Jeffrey Mishlove's *The Roots of Consciousness*; as well as the spirit entity-dictated volumes of *A Course in Miracles* by Dr. Helen Schucman.[362] In addition, Bernard Jensen's affinity with hardcore New Age pioneers like Helen Blavatsky and writers like Marilyn Ferguson and Helen Schucman casts a huge shadow over the credibility of his iridology theories.

Dr. George Goodheart—Founder of Applied Kinesiology

Dr. Goodheart was a chiropractor and a psychic who developed the art of applied kinesiology (AK), which is a blending of the theory and/or practice of the chiropractic and ancient Chinese Taoism. He believed "that every disease has a structural manifestation in a specific muscle weakness pattern,"[363] based on the same Taoist theory of universal energy, chi, which supposedly flows through the body's meridians. Here is a chiropractor incorporating occult divination into his practice.

Rudolf Steiner—founder of anthroposophical medicine

Rudolf Steiner, the founder of anthroposophical medicine, which is based on human wisdom and channeled messages from the spirits, was a clairvoyant necromancer (communicating with the spirits of the dead)[364] and an advocate of the New Age holistic approach. He was one of the first to investigate the apparent link between natural science and the spirit world. Steiner, like his contemporary, Edgar Cayce, prescribed homeopathic remedies revealed to him by the spirits.[365] He was also the founder of the Waldorf Schools, which were based on secular humanism and "emphasized color form, rhythm and the life of nature."[366] Clearly Rudolf Steiner used parapsychology as a clairvoyant necromancer. His ideas were synthesized from the Rosecrucians, Theosophical theories, Christian beliefs, and the occult.

Dr. Elmer Green and Dr. Alyce Green—biofeedback pioneers

Dr. Elmer Green "is known for the first real breakthrough toward a simple cure for migraine headache; he used the occult technique of biofeedback for it."[367] The Greens, who pioneered a biofeedback temperature device while working at the Menninger Clinic in the early 1960s, were, by their own admission, avid readers in the fields of metaphysics, parapsychology, and theosophy, searching for and constructing a framework of ideas that would correspond with our own experiences and at the same time be reasonable in terms of a possible science in which mind and matter were not forever separate.[368]

This is very apparent from the bibliography in their book *Beyond Biofeedback*, in which the Greens cite the writings of occult New Agers like Roberto Assagioli, Alice Bailey, Helen Blavatsky, Fritzjof Capra, and Carlos Casteneda.[369] Dr. Green also talked with and received advice from a spiritual "Teacher."[370] It is evident that the Drs. Green were heavily involved in the occult and parapsychology and brought elements of it into biofeedback.

Dolores Krieger and Dora Kunz—founders of therapeutic touch

New York University professor, Dolores Krieger, was the founder and original proponent of modern neopagan therapeutic touch (TT).[371] Dr. Krieger, a Buddhist, drew largely from the religious and healing philosophies of the Chinese, Hindus, and Native Americans.[372] She established her first center for TT in a Catholic-oriented school of nursing in the early 1970s and urged her students to "record their dreams, consult the I Ching and draw mandalas . . . symbolizing the unity of the soul with the universe" to aid them in meditation.[373]

Dora Kunz, on whose teachings Krieger built her hand-healing techniques, is a self-proclaimed psychic and clairvoyant who studied under the occultist Charles W. Leadbeater, whom Dolores Krieger called "the great seer of the twentieth century."[374] Kunz was also a "former president of the Theosophical Society in America."[375]

These New Age holistic health pioneers were into the occult, parapsychology, and the Eastern mystical religions. They were all drinking from polluted cisterns. The Bible says, "Doth a fountain send forth at the same place sweet water and bitter?" (James 3:11) and "Who can bring a clean thing out of an unclean? Not one" (Job 14:4).

It would be well to emphasize again that not only is New Age alternative medicine unscientific, but its pioneers were inspired by the dark world of the occult. Does this really matter if it works? Can we just pick out the good and leave the bad? In the next chapter the pragmatic approach will be discussed.

13

Pragmatism: Dangerous Reasoning

Pragmatism: "If it works . . ."

William James (1842–1910), "the most widely-read American philosopher of the 1900s," is credited with developing the philosophy of "pragmatism." James believed that "every person must make up his own mind on issues of human life and destiny that cannot be settled on scientific grounds."[376] According to his pragmatic philosophy, an idea or issue was considered valid solely upon the basis of its practical consequences. In other words, "if it works, use it." For millions today, this has become the undeclared criterion for determining what they do and why they do it.

Many things that "work" are not acceptable for Seventh-day Adventists. For example, the reason for refraining from eating unclean meats (dogs, cats, reptiles, shrimp, pork, and horses) is simply because God prohibited it (Leviticus 11). However, millions of people around the world partake of the "unclean" meats and apparently do well on them. Nevertheless, God has forbidden the consumption of these flesh foods.

The reason Adventists should not get involved in occult or spiritualistic activities, including New Age holistic health, is that they are based on nonbiblical philosophies, (clearly condemned in the Bible—Deut. 18:9-14) as well as in the inspired writings of Ellen White and share the same ideology as the New Age movement.

The Biblical Research Institute of the General Conference of Seventh-day Adventists, in a document entitled "The New Age Movement and Seventh-day Adventists," states that:

> God explicitly forbade Israel to adopt the occult techniques of the pagan Canaanites (Deut 18:9-14; Lev. 19:26). Consequently, we cannot see consistency in a Seventh-day Adventist Christian functioning like a holistic healer by using techniques and therapies that are the distinctive property of the occult-mystic program. Nothing can prevent the demonic powers from intruding into the processes to affect either the practitioner, the patient, or both.[377]

Just before the Israelites crossed over into the Promised Land, they were instructed to destroy the pagan idols of the nations they conquered. Not only that, they were also to avoid even recycling the gold or silver of which these idols were made.

> The graven images of their gods shall ye burn with fire: thou shalt not desire the silver or gold that is on them, nor take it unto thee, lest thou be snared therein: for it is an abomination to the Lord thy God. Neither shalt thou bring an abomination into thine house, lest thou be a cursed thing like it: but thou shalt utterly detest it, and thou shalt utterly abhor it; for it is a cursed thing (Deut. 7:25, 26).

This passage shows just how offensive to God the pagan systems are. One might argue, "What would be so wrong with melting down the golden idols and using the gold for some useful items or works of art? There was nothing wrong with the precious metal in itself, but the fact that it was a part of pagan worship condemned it. As you will recall, Moses did not melt down the golden calf at Mt. Sinai and use it for something "good." No; it was pulverized and poured into the drinking water. Those Israelites who had fallen into idolatry over the golden calf were forced to drink it and the gold ended up in human excrement on the desert floor. The principle here holds true with holistic health therapies associated with pagan philosophies. God abhors everything associated with pagan worldview philosophies and practices.

The placebo effect

Some New Age holistic health therapies work on a "placebo" basis. Generally, a placebo is "a harmless, unmedicated preparation given as a medicine to a patient merely to humor him."[378] Any benefit gained comes through the power of suggestion. In other words, some people place so much confidence in a New Age practitioner and/or remedy (like homeopathy) that, psychologically, the treatment makes them feel better even though without the therapy they probably would have gotten better with the passing of time. "For many years doctors have observed that placebos (inactive substances administered to patients) often prove as effective as active medicine."[379]

Patients who are "open-minded," "receptive," and "susceptible" to these New Age alternative remedies are more prone to the placebo effect than others who are not. Let us remember also that many physical illnesses and injuries are healed in time by the body's own healing system. Normally a cut on the finger, for instance, will heal with a little TLC (tender loving care) and time. The point is that New Age holistic health practitioners sometimes get the credit for what the body's natural healing system does.

Dangerous reasoning

Some Christians would argue that if their so-called holistic health therapies and remedies can restore one's health, it is all right to use them, regardless of their questionable ties to mysticism, their unscientific basis, and their practitioner's nonbiblical worldview. Some would attempt to justify their course of action with New Age holistic health by declaring that yin and yang mean nothing to them, and they could care less what Samuel Hahnemann and Dolores Krieger believed in. All they know is that they were once ill and in pain, and now they are well. And that's good enough for them. Or, if they do recognize the questionable pagan elements in those therapies and practices, they feel they can extract the "good" therapies and practices from the "bad," nonbiblical philosophies upon which they are based. But in terms of New Age holistic health, is pragmatism a good course of action for God-fearing people? I hardly think so, for the apostle Paul states in 1 Corinthians 10:21, 22 that "You cannot drink the cup of the Lord and the cup of demons too; you cannot have a part in both the Lord's table and the table of demons. Are we trying to arouse the Lord's jealousy? Are we stronger than he?"

The obvious answer to the first question Paul asked is Yes. We provoke the Lord to jealousy by fraternizing with the enemy. The answer to the second question is definitely No because we are not stronger than God so as to think we can treat ourselves with therapies and remedies that were not inspired by God, but by the enemy. The Adventist health and healing philosophy includes the concept that Christ is the Great Physician. And the true Healer does not work through modern-day shamans or New Age holistic health doctors. Our concern should not be solely for the healing. There should be equal concern for the fact that there is a spiritual danger in New Age holistic health of which Christians should be aware.

The Biblical Research Institute of the General Conference of Seventh-day Adventists (BRI), in "The New Age Movement and Seventh-day Adventists" states (to quote the BRI document again) that:

> It is dangerous reasoning for Christians to think that they can *adopt and adapt cult healing techniques and separate them from their original context—as though healing rested in the technique only,* a procedure which at times may be irrational in itself. We question whether an occult practice can be superimposed upon a Christian base without bringing the patient (in time) a false worldview or making such persons liable to oppression from the demonic powers who originated the cult-mystical practice in the first place[380] (italics added).

Would it make it "kosher" if an Adventist physician incorporated acupuncture, applied kinesiology, or homeopathy into his practice? Not according to Dr. Jochen Hawlischek, Health and Temperance Director for the Euro-African Division of Seventh-day Adventists:

> Astrology, yoga, yin-yang, acupuncture, iridology, homeopathy, reflexology, pendulum, etc. have no scientific basis. They are based on the oriental pantheistic con-

ception of a cosmic energy, or magnetic fluid, where the human being is part of the cosmos and the restoration of the imbalance of this fluid would bring the person back into harmony with this universal energy—god. . . . *The fact that a sincere Christian physician utilizes such methods of healing does not sanctify them*[381] (italics added).

The BRI document on New Age addresses the pragmatic thinking of many Christians by again asking "Can the Christian safely adopt these procedures by cutting away their roots?" The answer:

> We repeat an earlier observation: God explicitly forbade Israel to adopt the occult techniques of the pagan Canaanites (Deut. 18:9-14; Lev. 19:26). Consequently we cannot see consistency in a Seventh-day Adventist Christian functioning like a holistic healer by using techniques and therapies that are the distinctive property of the occult-mystic program. Nothing can prevent the demonic powers from intruding into the processes to affect either the practitioner, the patient, or both.[382]

In our own Sabbath School quarterly for the first quarter of 1989, Dr. Leslie Hardinge and Frank Holbrook underlined the grave danger of pragmatic thinking regarding New Age holistic health:

> Psychic healing, often employing the use of the pendulum or other objects to diagnose and treat disease, has long been an integral part of the occult. *All the occultic Eastern methods of treating disease and stress* are tied to the non-biblical pantheistic world view of reality. There are attempts at times to keep this fact hidden. *It is dangerous for Christians to think that they can borrow and adapt the healing procedures of the occult. The attempt to give occult practices a Christian veneer opens the door to satanic delusion and oppression*[383] (italics added).

The Health and Temperance Director for the General Conference, Dr. Albert Whiting, has stated very succinctly that

> Examples of alternative forms of treatment that must

be rejected include *homeopathy, reflexology, iridology, pendulum therapy,* and *treatments associated with spurious philosophies of astrology, yoga, yin-yang,* and *spiritism.* These are not only unproven but are totally irrational from an understanding of human anatomy and physiology. Those associated with psychic phenomena have serious spiritual implications.[384]

Dr. John Harvey Kellogg's criteria still valid

Dr. John Harvey Kellogg, one of the most prominent and famous physicians that Adventism has produced, was the director of the Sanitarium in Battle Creek, Michigan in the early 1900s. By 1929, the Battle Creek Sanitarium (affectionately known as the "San") had grown from a one-patient sanitarium at its opening to 1,200 patients. It had achieved international recognition, being patronized by United States president William Howard Taft, royalty, and other famous personages such as John D. Rockefeller, J. C. Penney, Dale Carnegie, Amelia Earhart and Billy Sunday.[385]

In his heyday, Dr. Kellogg one day asked his colleague, Dr. Paulson, if he (Paulson) had any idea why he (Kellogg) and the San generally stayed five years ahead of the rest of the medical profession of his day. Paulson replied that he didn't know. At that, Kellogg told him:

> When a new thing is brought out in the medical world I know from my knowledge of the Spirit of Prophecy whether it belongs in our [Seventh-day Adventist] system or not. If it does, I instantly adopt it and advertise it while the rest of the doctors are slowly feeling their way, and when they finally adopt it, I have five years' start on them. On the other hand, when the medical profession is swept off their feet by some new fad, if it does not fit the light we have received, I simply do not touch it. When the doctors finally discover their mistake, they wonder how it came that I did not get caught.[386]

The same criteria that Kellogg used during his time for testing new medical discoveries or alternative therapies could and should be the same criteria that Seventh-day Adventists use to test alternative therapies and practices today. If they don't "square" with the Bible and the Spirit of Prophecy, we should simply not touch them. Speaking of the Spirit of Prophecy, the writings of E. G. White contain some cautions and warnings that would be well to look at.

Warnings and cautions from the Spirit of Prophecy

Even though the phrase "New Age" had not yet been coined in Ellen White's time, she used the term "modern spiritualism" to describe the same phenomena. Ellen White was well acquainted with the spurious alternative therapies and remedies that were prevalent in her day, such as Christian Science (mind/body medicine), homeopathy, phrenology, the theories of animal magnetism, the Emmanuel movement (treatments directed toward the subconscious), Oriental healing practices, and electric and magnetic healers of all sorts. Some of these were forerunners of New Age holistic health therapies and remedies that have become popular in the last two decades while others are still in vogue today.

In the following quotations notice the warnings regarding the spiritual dangers connected with these forms of healing that still apply today. In *Evangelism*, chapter 18, pages 606-609, under the subtitle "Christian Science, Oriental and Healing Cults," Ellen White says,

> There are many who shrink with horror from the thought of consulting spirit mediums, but who are attracted by *more pleasing forms of spiritism*, such as the Emmanuel movement. Still others are led astray by the teachings of Christian Science, and by the mysticism of theosophy and *other Oriental religions*.
>
> The apostles of nearly all forms of spiritism claim to have the power to cure the diseased. They attribute their power to electricity, magnetism, the so-called "sympathetic remedies," or to latent forces within the mind of man. And there are not a few, even in this Christian age, who go to these healers, instead of *trusting in the power of the living God and the skill of well-qualified Christian physicians.*

Angels of God will preserve His people while they walk in the path of duty; but there is *no assurance of such protection for those who deliberately venture upon Satan's ground.* An agent of the great deceiver will say and do anything to gain his object. It matters little whether he calls himself a spiritualist, an "electric physician," or a "magnetic healer."

These satanic agents claim to cure disease. They attribute their power to electricity, magnetism, or the so-called "sympathetic remedies," *while in truth they are but channels for Satan's electric currents. By this means he casts his spell over the bodies and souls of men* (italics added).[387]

The mother, watching by the sickbed of her child, exclaims, "I can do no more! Is there no physician who has power to restore my child!" She is told of the wonderful cures performed by some clairvoyant or magnetic healer, and she trusts her dear one to his charge, *placing it as verily in the hand of Satan as if he were standing by her side. In many instances the future life of the child is controlled by a satanic power which it seems impossible to break* (italics added).[388]

The above passages strongly support the fact that there is real spiritual danger in putting yourself in the hands of practitioners or physicians who employ these spurious types of health care.

The Mosaic health code

When God gave Moses the instructions for prevention of disease and maintenance of good health, He did not allow Moses to incorporate into them a single medical remedy that was used in Egypt or Mesopotamia even though their medical science was greatly developed and Moses had even been schooled in that knowledge (Acts 7:22). God would not permit any mixture of the occult with the divine. And God has not changed. He is still the same today as He was yesterday and as He will be tomorrow. God desires His people to separate from all pagan, nonbiblical worldview philosophies and practices, including those used for health purposes. Instead, the Mosaic Code includes principles on hygiene, diet, prevention of disease, quarantine, etc. And Adventists not only benefit from these biblical principles in the Pentateuch but also from the eight natural remedies given in the Spirit of Prophecy:

> Pure air, sunlight, abstemiousness, rest, exercise, proper diet, the use of water, trust in divine power—these are the true remedies. Every person should have a knowledge of nature's remedial agencies and how to apply them. It is essential both to understand the principles involved in the treatment of the sick and to have a practical training that will enable one rightly to use this knowledge.[389]

And last but not least, we are to trust in the skill of well-qualified Christian physicians (*Evangelism*, p. 606)—all of which gives Christians a health care package second to none.

God's call to separate

God has always called His people to separate from the occult and pagan customs and practices of the world. One of the strongest commandments to have nothing to do with them is found in Deuteronomy: "There shall not be found among you any one that maketh his son or his daughter to pass through the fire, or that useth *divination*, or an *observer of times*, or an *enchanter*, or a *witch*, or a *charmer*, or a *consulter with familiar spirits*, or a *wizard*, or a *necromancer*" (Deut 18:10, 11, italics added).

Paul's second letter to the Corinthians contains an equally strong commandment:

> Be ye not unequally yoked together with unbelievers; for what fellowship hath righteousness with unrighteousness? and what communion hath light with darkness? And what concord hath Christ with Belial? or what part hath he that believeth with an infidel? And what agreement hath the temple of God with idols? for ye are the temple of the living God; as God hath said, I will dwell in them, and walk in them; and I will be their God and they shall be my people. *Wherefore come out from among them and be ye separate, saith*

the Lord, and touch not the unclean thing, and I will receive you (2 Cor 6:14-17).

God's reason for admonishing His people to remain separate from pagan practice is because He wants us to be perfect (Deut 18:12) and totally dedicated to Him. If we are engaging in anything that is tainted with paganism or occultism, we cannot be perfect in Him. Christ desires to have a glorious, holy church as His bride without spot, wrinkle, or blemish (Eph. 5:27).

Why holistic health is forbidden ground

Why are the alternative New Age holistic health therapies and remedies that are connected in some way with the occult or paganism forbidden ground for Seventh-day Adventists?

1. They are based on nonbiblical worldviews.

New Age holistic health therapies and remedies are based on nonbiblical worldviews such as monism, pantheism, animism, and naturalism, which are all diametrically opposed to the true biblical theist worldview.

The Christian theistic worldview teaches that this world's peace and harmony were broken when a "little sin" (partaking of forbidden fruit) plunged the human race into degradation and separation from God the Creator. The tree of knowledge of good and evil contained "good" as well as "evil," and God forbade Adam and Eve to eat of it because mixing good and evil results not in peace, harmony, and well-being, but in separation from God, degeneration, and death. The only way to return to the Edenic state of peace and harmony that existed before the Fall is for God to completely eradicate sin from this planet. In God's economy, peace and harmony are not a result of the balancing of universal negative and positive forces, but are rather a total eradication of evil and man's total submission to God's holy will.

None of the nonbiblical worldviews teaches that God is the Creator and Sustainer of the universe and the earth. None teaches that He is a personal God who loves and cares for His creatures. None of the worldviews has a correct concept of the nature of man, sin, retribution, death, and redemption. It is only the biblical theist view that presents the fallen human race as in need of a Saviour. It is only the theist view that recognizes Christ as the Son of God who came to live and give His life as a ransom for our salvation. The Adventist philosophy of health and healing is based on this premise and is a part of God's plan of restoration and redemption.

The New Age movement presents a serious challenge to Christians because its worldview is unbiblical. Yet its emphasis on holistic health has led many Christians, including some Seventh-day Adventists, to adopt certain techniques and therapies. The bewildering array of techniques, therapies, and seminars and workshops—some of which appear quite neutral in tone—has produced confusion in Christian circles about whether the holistic health aspect of the movement would be dangerous to Christian faith and experience. As in most deceptions, truth and error are mixed in varying proportions.[390]

2. They were founded by pioneers in the occult.

Many of the recent New Age holistic health pioneers were involved in the parapsychology movement such as the Theosophical Society, psychic phenomena, and spiritism. These pioneers, by and large, nurtured their thinking with polluted and occult pagan concepts. The Bible says, "Doth a fountain send forth at the same place sweet water and bitter?" (James 3:11); and "Who can bring a clean thing out of an unclean? Not one" (Job 14:4).

3. God disapproves of them.

God has explicitly forbidden His people to participate in any occult or pagan practices (Deut. 18:9-14; 12:1-4) and has given instructions that forbid involvement with pagans (2 Cor. 6:14-17). His church is to be holy, without blemish (Rev. 18:4; Eph. 5:27).

Neither God nor Christ works with healers who employ nonbiblical worldviews and occult therapies and health remedies. The Adventist health and healing philosophy is that Christ is the Great Physician and He works with physicians and practitioners who employ the anatomical, physiological and natural laws of health.

The "three strike" principle can easily be applied here. Why are New Age holistic health therapies off-limits for Christians? Because:

1. They are based on non-biblical worldviews—Strike One!

2. Their pioneers were into the occult———Strike Two!

3. They are an abomination to God———Strike Three!!!!THEY ARE OUT!!!

Is there no God in Israel?

The story goes that one of the Jewish kings, Ahaziah, fell from his balcony and his injuries became life threatening. In his desperation, he sent one of his servants to consult the neighboring pagan god, Baal, whether he would live or die. God, who was certainly offended by this course of action, sent his prophet, Elisha, to intercept the king's messenger and ask him a very thought-provoking question, "Is it because there is no God in Israel for you to consult that you have sent messengers to consult Baal-Zebub?" (NIV) So many Christian people, like King Ahaziah, just "don't get it." God is not pleased when we consult with healers who employ nonbiblical worldview methods of healing. The king's insistence on finding out about his illness, in the process, sacrificed two captains and 100 soldiers. Finally, the prophet went to the king and communicated God's disapproval and sentence of death for him for fraternizing with the enemy (2 Kings 1:1-18). The principle is clear, we are not to consult with, much less be treated by, those who practice alternative forms of healing based on worldviews that do not recognize God as the only sovereign God in the universe.

The same thought-provoking question could be and should be asked today when the urge or the temptation comes to see a New Age holistic healer, whether he be a medical doctor or just a practitioner. "Is there no God in Israel?" The answer is "Yes, there is." Then why do we want to go to New Age holistic health/medicine practitioners?

Two healing powers

There are two healing powers in this world: the divine healing power of God and the demonic healing power of Satan. Both the Bible and the Spirit of Prophecy affirm that God is the only true Healer.

The Biblical Research Institute document on "The New Age Movement and Seventh-day Adventists" states that both God and Satan can heal.

> There is no question that healings take place with the use of occult methods. That is what makes them deceptive. We have observed already that according to the Bible the dark powers are well able to work miracles and to do wonders. It is not in the healing or the miracle that the evidence is to be sought. *Both God and Satan can heal.* Consequently, the Christian must look beyond the miracle or healing to the teachings being endorsed. Healing by occult-mystical methods simply endorses the occult-mystical world view and places both the practitioner and the patient on Satan's ground to be oppressed by him at will[391] (italics added).

It should come then as no surprise that Satan is also able to heal.[392] After all, he is the cause of, or is indirectly responsible for, all the pain and sickness in the world. For more than 6000 years he has studied the human race and all its facets—psychological, physiological, anatomical, and spiritual. He knows all about us, inside and out. In some cases he makes people sick and then removes the sickness, making it appear that he has healed them.[393]

Shamans and witch doctors in the developing countries can, without ever touching the sick person, heal them of their fever and abdominal disorders just by pronouncing mantras (using repeated phrases) as they shake a branch of a "sacred" bush around the seated or bedridden patient's body. I ask, "What supernatural healing power did the healing?" It is obvious that it was not the divine healing power of God.

> Through spiritualism, Satan appears as a benefactor of the race, healing the diseases of the people and professing to present a new and more exalted system of religious faith; but at the same time he works as a destroyer.[394]

Seventh-day Adventists always need to ask one more question beyond "Does it work?" They need to ask, "*Who* makes it work?" and then base their course of action upon the answer.

14

Summary of New Age Holistic Health

Since the subject matter of New Age alternative medicine is technical, a comprehensive summary may be helpful.

1. Holistic Health and New Age share same goals

Alternative New Age holistic health is associated with the New Age movement because they both share the same metaphysical and philosophical goals and beliefs, such as the ushering in of a new age, the existence of invisible universal energies operating in the human body, astrology and teachings of the Eastern mystical religions. Both the New Age movement and New Age holistic health share the ultimate goal of personal and social "transformation" from the current paradigms to the New Age paradigm.

2. Portrayed as "natural" and "harmless"

New Age holistic health can be alluring and at the same time deceiving to Seventh-day Adventists because New Age holistic health therapies and practices are promoted as "natural," "holistic," "noninvasive," and because the patient participates in the healing process. For the uninformed and unsuspecting Christian, alternative New Age holistic health and true Adventist wholistic health can appear to be natural and harmless.

3. Metaphysical spirituality

When New Agers and New Age holistic health practitioners talk about "spirit" or "spiritual" as one of the three components of holistic health, they are referring to "inward spirituality" and connecting with supernatural entities, not to biblical spirituality.

4. A pathway into the New Age movement

New Age holistic health can be a pathway into the New Age movement for Adventists and non-Adventists alike who have given up on conventional medicine or who have been given up on by conventional medicine.

5. Influenced by monistic worldview

New Age holistic health has been greatly influenced by traditional Chinese medicine and by the philosophies upon which it is founded; namely, the monistic worldview.

6. Universal energy common denominator

Applied kinesiology is a pseudoscience based on the manipulation of the mysterious universal energies called "chi" by the Chinese, "prana" by the Hindus, "mana" by the Hawaiians, "innate" by D. D. Palmer, and used to diagnose the condition of the vital organs of the body through muscle testing.

Other energy-manipulating New Age therapies, such as therapeutic touch, reflexology, Shiatsu, and acupressure, are based on the same theory of "chi" among the Chinese and "prana" among the Hindus. This energy has not been scientifically isolated or proven. In therapeutic touch, the practitioner does not even touch the patient to move the universal energy, but is dependent on mystical forces operating through the practitioner's hands, which is not according to the physiological laws of the body.

7. Influenced by pantheistic worldview

New Age holistic health has also been influenced by Hindu ayurvedic medicine, which is based on a pantheistic worldview, the philosophy that every part of the universe is a living manifestation of God, that an essence of God is in everything that exists.

Therapies and practices, such as aromatherapy and homeopathy, are also based on the oriental religious philosophy of pantheism, which attributes spirit energy to natural remedies derived from flowers, plants, minerals, or animal products. This worldview does away with a personal, living God who created the earth and continues to sustain it.

8. Employs Eastern mystical meditation

Ayurvedic medicine employs occult altered states of consciousness (a form of self-hypnosis) through mystical meditation associated with yogis and shamans. Altered states of consciousness are said to be avenues to self-awareness, to one's higher self and connectedness to "spirit masters," involving *asanas* (meditative positions), rhythmic breathing techniques, "centering," the use of mandalas and mantras. "Spirit masters" include Hindu gods, angels, deceased shamans, and the spirits of great men and women. Communicating with the dead is strongly condemned by the Bible (Deut. 18:10, 11). Altered states of consciousness and visualization techniques are spiritually dangerous because the individual opens up his subconscious mind to possible demonic influence.

9. Iridology influenced by Hindu chakras

The iris of the eye, contrary to what is taught by iridologists, is not the nerve center for the whole body, nor is it the roadmap to the body. Iridology is unreliable because it involves much guesswork (divination) on the part of practitioners and because it shares many of the mystical concepts of Hindu chakra energy fields.

10. Pendulum divination is occult

Pendulum divination is closely related to the ancient practice of dowsing and is based strictly on occult divination, which is prohibited in the Bible.

11. Holistic health pioneers into occult

The recent holistic health pioneers and developers of many of the New Age holistic health therapies and practices were greatly influenced by the Eastern mystical religions, such as Hinduism and Buddhism. They were either associated with the Theosophical Society, involved in the parapsychology phenomena, or contacted and communicated with disembodied universal entities.

12. Defiling the body temple with pagan therapies

Defiling the body temple involves a moral principle as much as it does a physical one. God is "jealous" when we allow ourselves to be treated by therapies and practices that are associated with pagan and occult beliefs.

13. Mosaic health code free from pagan practices

Even though both the Egyptian and the Mesopotamian civilizations by the time of Moses had developed a "science" of medicine, God did not allow Moses to incorporate any of their therapies, practices, or remedies into the preventive health instructions given to the Israelites.

14. Eight "natural" or "true" remedies

The eight natural or true remedies—nutrition, exercise, pure water, sunlight, temperance, pure air, rest, and trust in God— that God provided in the Garden of Eden to maintain optimum health of mind and body remain and are recommended by the Spirit of Prophecy for the health and well-being of everyone today.

Criteria for Measuring Biblical and Spirit of Prophecy-Approved "Natural" and "Wholistic" Therapies

The following criteria should be applied to any questionable alternative therapy or remedy:

1. Is it based on a theistic, biblical worldview? If the therapy or remedy is derived from traditional Chinese medicine or Ayurvedic medicine, or has anything to do with the so-called "universal ener-

gies" such as Chi, Qi, Ki (Yin and Yang), prana, mana, etc., be assured that these therapies and remedies are not based on a theistic, biblical worldview.

2. Apply the Seventh-day Adventist health philosophy to the therapy or remedy. Does the practitioner consider himself/herself to be a co-worker with the Great Physician, Jesus Christ?

3. Do the therapies work according to the anatomical and physiological functions of the human body?

4. Is an altered state of consciousness, introspective type of meditation (such as Eastern meditation, yoga, or TM) a part of the therapy? Is imaging or visualizing a part of the therapy?

5. Are the practitioners credible and bonded? What are their credentials? What has their track record been? Are they involved in parapsychology or astrology?

6. Do they operate out of a New Age holistic wellness center? What kind of literature is at the disposal of the waiting patients? What other therapies of a questionable nature are offered at the wellness center? Do they play New Age meditative instrumental music (only harmony sounds with no rhythm, beat, or distinguishable melody) in the background?

7. What other therapies are offered and practiced by the practitioner? For instance, are acupuncture, acupressure, applied kinesiology, Shiatsu, iridology, reflexology, homeopathy, chakra balancing, aura readings, or divination techniques offered?

8. Herbs should be taken with sufficient understanding of their medicinal values, in moderation, and in their natural state when possible. Some herbs are toxic or poisonous in themselves, while others are harmful when blended with those that are not complementary to them. Homeopathic natural remedies that include herb substances are a misnomer, since in most homeopathic remedies not even one single molecule of the original substance is believed to be present in the medicine. The healing effect is attributed to the "spirit" or "essence" that is left after the vigorous shakings and astronomical dilutions.

9. Any therapy which has to do with "divination," whether it be

dowsing, use of the pendulum, or applied kinesiology, is vehemently condemned in the Bible (Deut 18:9-14).

10. Any therapy that has to do with a psychic or a seer or fortuneteller, such as a palm reader, tarot card reader, or astrological sign reader, is condemned in the Bible (Deut 18:9-14).

11. The New Age massage therapies, with the exception of Shiatsu (which is based on acupuncture points), use the "centrifugal" technique, which claims to move vital energy from the center of the body to the extremities and sometimes out of the body. The more acceptable forms of massage are those that employ the "centripetal" technique, which works with the circulatory system to promote good circulation of the blood from the extremities back to the heart, where it is purified and recirculated. "Centrifugal" modalities of massage employed by the New Age holistic health therapist, on the other hand, move alleged congested "energy" from the center of the body outward to the extremities. Negative energy is supposedly moved completely out of the body.

15

Witnessing to the New Ager

Do you have a friend who is into tarot cards and psychics? Are you a parent whose son or daughter is caught up with Wicca, the occult on the Internet, martial arts, or Eastern meditation? Are your friends using homeopathic medicine or having their allergies tested with applied kinesiology? Do you know someone who is talking to or receiving messages from their "guardian angel" or another spirit guide? If so, and you would like to witness to them, read on. This chapter is especially for you.

Remember, some people who are involved in the New Age are sincere Christians who, without even realizing it, are participating in or receiving therapies associated with the New Age.

There are those that join the New Age environmental movements because they want to help solve the world's pollution and hunger problems. Others that wind up in the New Age movement are there because they were dissatisfied with their Christian faith and were out seeking for spiritual meaning and satisfaction in their lives. Still others are deeply into the New Age, because they think they can extract the practice or therapy without being in danger of spiritualistic consequences.

Not all New Agers believe everything there is in the New Age movement or belong to New Age organizations. Most New Agers just pick and choose what "turns them on." So before you start witnessing to your friend or family member, find out what area of the New Age they are into.

Preparation for witnessing to a New Ager

The following are things that you should concern yourself with before witnessing or giving Bible studies to a New Ager:

1. Know what you believe.

"All whose faith is not firmly established upon the word of God will be deceived and overcome."[395] Make sure you have a good understanding of Seventh-day Adventist church doctrines, especially:

A. Creation and the Christian theistic worldview

B. The nature of God

C. The nature of man and the state of the dead

D. How sin entered the world and its consequences

E. Biblical condemnation of spiritualism and the occult

F. The plan of salvation

G. How to lead a person to Jesus Christ

H. The judgment

I. The second coming of Christ

J. The earth made new

2. Pray for protection.

Pray that God will use you to bring your friend or family member out of the New Age. Intercede with God on behalf of this person. Ask God to put a burden on your heart for him or her, praying for him or her several times during the day. Then pray for your own spiritual protection as you work with this individual.

The admonition that the apostle Paul gave the Ephesians (Eph. 6:10-17) penned from his Roman prison cell in AD 62, is more relevant and meaningful today than ever before.

> Finally, my brethren, be strong in the Lord, and in the power of his might. Put on the whole armor of God, that ye may be able to stand against the wiles of the devil. For we wrestle not against flesh and blood, but against principalities, against powers, against the rulers of the

darkness of this world, against spiritual wickedness in high places. Wherefore take unto you the whole armor of God, that ye may be able to withstand in the evil day, and having done all, to stand. Stand therefore, having your loins girt about with truth, and having on the breastplate of righteousness. And your feet shod with the preparation of the gospel of peace; Above all, taking the shield of faith wherewith ye shall be able to quench all the fiery darts of the wicked. And take the helmet of salvation and the sword of the Spirit, which is the word of God.

As Christian warriors in the final showdown, God has not left us unprepared. He has provided His suit of armor calculated to defend us from the cunning and subtle attacks of Satan that otherwise would destroy us. The spiritualistic struggle between the good forces of Christ and the evil forces of Satan is real. This battle for our souls is not being fought with physical foes, but rather with a cosmic host of demons that work best in the paranormal metaphysical realms of mystical human experience.

Therefore, we need to put on the whole armor of God in a prayerful attitude (v. 18), starting with the belt of truth, which is the Word of God. The bulletproof vest of Christ's righteousness. The combat boots of the gospel, that "God so loved the world, that, He gave His only begotten son, that whosoever believeth in Him should not perish, but have everlasting life" (John 3:16). The shield of faith that makes it possible to have full confidence and trust in God. The helmet of salvation that gives us the assurance that we are His. And last, the sharp and shining sword of God's Spirit that will bring conviction to the heart of those we are working for. Not one piece of God's armor can be ignored or disregarded. They're all important. A half-armored soldier is preparing him or herself for defeat and/or failure. The enemy will surely find your weakest spot and attack you there. God's armor is guaranteed to protect you completely.

Commenting on Ephesians 6:12, Ellen White says:

Those who oppose the teachings of spiritualism are assailing, not men alone, but Satan and his angels. They have entered upon a contest against principalities and powers and wicked spirits in high places. Satan will not yield one inch of ground except as he is driven back by the power of heavenly messengers.[396]

3. Target the area of New Age error.

If you don't already know what area of the New Age your friend or relative is into, find out. You can do this by asking them many questions about what they believe. This will not only help you know where they're coming from but will help them to see some of the fallacies of what they have espoused.

Most New Age philosophies, beliefs and practices are based on Eastern pantheism. Pantheism (*pan* meaning "all," everything in the Universe, and *theism*, meaning "god/universal force")

Pantheism teaches that the universe and everything in it is god or is a manifestation of god. In pantheism there is no personal, living God that sustains and intervenes in the affairs of the human race. Our Creator-God is apart from creation, while the pantheistic god is one with creation. Their god is in everything: in the leaf of the trees, in the blade of grass, in the raindrop, and in human beings. Thus we are gods.

4. Acquaint yourself briefly with the subject matter.

There are several excellent books written against the New Age by Christians, including some Adventist authors such as Will Baron, Kenneth Wade, and David Marshall. Their books can be purchased at your local Adventist Book Center. Also the Sabbath School/Personal Ministries Department of the General Conference has a series of 20 books entitled "Reaching Special People," one of which I authored on the New Age. That book contains an excellent glossary, a nearly exhaustive list of beliefs and practices which are considered "New Age," along with Bible Study outlines to use when working with people who are caught up in this last-day deception.

Review the chapters in this book that deal with these areas of New Age deceptive beliefs and practices or check out a book from the library on the topic of their interest. Caution should be exercised if you are going to read "hard-core" books on these subjects because the New Age is spiritually dangerous. Be careful. All you need is a brief understanding so you can approach him on an intelligent level. If you are dealing with a sincere but naïve Christian caught up in the New Age, you can freely use all the Bible and Spirit of Prophecy teachings you want against these nonbiblical worldviews and practices.

5. Become their friend.

Befriend them without compromising. Resist the temptation of accepting invitations to New Age gatherings, even out of mere curiosity. Some have done so and it has taken days and weeks and even years to get rid of annoying and tormenting evil spirit effects. You can't hope to gain the confidence of a person caught up in the New Age until they feel that you really care—that you are sincere and love them.

6. Uplift Christ.

As much as possible, exhibit Christ's love to them. Ellen White states, that "The last rays of merciful light, the last message of mercy to be given to the world, is a revelation of His character of love."[397] This can only happen as we show them Christ's love in our lives. You will find that many New Agers accept Jesus Christ as a guru to the Christians, much like Gandhi was to the Hindus. What they don't accept is Jesus as their personal Saviour, and that's what you will need to work on.

Some New Agers want to get out of this demonic movement but don't know how or can't because they don't have the power to do so. These need to see the reality of their situation as captives of Satan's spiritual powers. For these, hold up Christ as the only One who can cut them loose from the grips of the devil.

"For this purpose the Son of God was manifested, that he might destroy the works of the devil" 1 John 3:8.

New Agers need to see Jesus as their Friend and Saviour. Jesus Himself said "If I, if I be lifted up from the earth, will draw all men unto me" John 12:32.

7. Give the truth in love.

The most effective way of dealing with error and evil is with the truth, the Bible. This is the method Jesus used when He confronted the devil. He always used a "Thus saith the Lord." If the person is sincere and is seeking for truth, they won't argue against the Word of God. However, when using the Scriptures against New Age beliefs, they cannot just be used in an authoritative way. They have to be given in love. Christian love expressed and demonstrated will break down many barriers that nothing else can.

CONCLUSION

Most New Agers, and especially the innocent followers of the Aquarian Conspiracy, do not understand the movement's ultimate objectives and goals of a utopian society. Nor do they know who masterminded this subtle last-day deception. As people are led to reject the truth, they will believe a lie (2 Thess. 2:10, 11). This will bring more spiritual darkness into our world. Our job is to let our light shine with the truth and love of Christ to dispel the darkness of error in the hearts and minds of people for whom Jesus died. May God give you wisdom, discernment, and power as you battle for those who have been caught up in Satan's deception.

16

The Last Great Deception

In reading and thinking about what is to take place just before Christ's second coming, and the prophesied attempt by Satan to deceive God's people by impersonating Christ, I came up with the following scenario.

Possible Scenario

With hands raised heavenward, he commanded huge balls of flashing fire, exploding with lightning power, to fall from the sky. Moments later, above the confusion, his melodious voice was heard:

"Peace, beloved. Fear not. I am your benefactor. I am—the Messiah. I am—Christ. I am—Krishna. I am—Buddha. I am Imam Mahdi. I am Lord Maitreya. I've been alive forever. I am the spark of all transcendental meditation thought. I understand your desire to bring everlasting peace to your planet, to eradicate poverty from the land, to preserve Gaia, Mother Earth, and to form a one-world religion."

These were the astonishing pronouncements made by Lord Maitreya, the long-awaited Messiah, who appeared like a dazzling and majestic angel of light and glory. Yesterday at noon he addressed a record crowd of 1.5 million surrounding the reflecting pool and the steps of the Lincoln Memorial in Washington, D.C. The day before, at the same hour, he appeared in front of the Los Angeles City Hall, where a crowd of 225,000 jammed the sidewalks and streets, jostling to get a closer look at this supernatural being who has the power to heal the sick and terminally ill, including those with AIDS.

All four of the major news networks (ABC, CBS, NBC, CNN) reported on their evening news that the Messiah was seen by record crowds in Rome, Calcutta, Beijing, Mexico City and Nairobi. His message is one of universal love, self-realization, global brotherhood, and spiritual oneness with Gaia, the spirit of Mother Earth. He advocates a unified form of worldwide spirituality for all people, encompassing the good of all religions and proclaiming Sunday as the sacred day for all to keep. The nation and the world stand in awe of this majestic one who at last has brought hope and healing to a world on the road to self-destruction. World leaders are in agreement that this amazing being of wisdom should be elevated to head the New World Order at the United Nations.

If you think this scenario is too far fetched, read for yourself an inspired composite account of this prophetic deception in *The Great Controversy* and other Spirit of Prophecy books where the impersonation of Christ is portrayed as Satan's crowning act of deception, "the strong, almost overmastering delusion."

As the crowning act in the great drama of deception, Satan himself will personate Christ. The church has long professed to look to the Saviour's advent as the consummation of her hopes. Now the great deceiver will make it appear that Christ has come. In different parts of the earth, Satan will manifest himself among men as a majestic being of dazzling brightness, resembling the description of the Son of God given by John in the Revelation.

The shout of triumph rings out upon the air: "Christ has come! Christ has come!" The people prostrate themselves in adoration before him, while he lifts up his hands and pronounces a blessing upon them, as Christ blessed His disciples when He was upon the earth. His voice is soft and subdued, yet full of melody. In gentle, compassionate tones he presents some of the same gracious, heavenly truths which the Saviour uttered; he heals the diseases of the people, and then, in his assumed character of Christ, he claims to have changed the Sabbath to Sunday, and commands all to hallow the day which he has blessed.

He declares that those who persist in keeping holy the seventh day are blaspheming his name by refusing to listen to his angels sent to them with light and truth. This is *the strong, almost overmastering delusion.*"[398] (italics added)

Why will it be an almost overmastering delusion? Because the major religions of the world are all waiting for a supernatural Messiah!

All major religions waiting for a "Messiah"

Take this for example, most of Christendom believes in a second coming of Christ. The Jewish people, since the beginning of time, have been waiting for their "Messiah." Muslims have been led to believe that Imam Mahdi will come again at this time. The Hindus believe that the time has come for the coming of the ninth reincarnation of Krishna. Buddhists wait for the fifth reincarnation of Buddha, while some New Agers are anticipating the emergence of Lord Maitreya, who is a composite of the saviours of all religious hopes and aspirations.

In the 1960s, when our nation went through a counter-cultural revolution, casting off the traditional Judeo-Christian values, many young people began looking to the East for spirituality and wisdom. Once-foreign and forbidden philosophies and practices of Eastern mystical religions (Deuteronomy 18:9-14) became prevalent in the West. The importation of spiritualistic teachings of pantheism, reincarnation, and concepts that humans are gods and can communicate with spiritual entities of the universe found an open market. Society is preoccupied with the subtle spiritualistic philosophies of "self": self-love, self-discovery, self-determination. People are intrigued and led to experiment with not-so-subtle spiritualistic psychics, channelers, and astrologers—perhaps because they promise not only to disclose the future but offer solutions for daily problems. The Spirit of Prophecy says that

Satan has long been preparing for his final effort to

deceive the world. The foundation of his work was laid by the assurance given to Eve in Eden: "Ye shall not surely die.". . .Little by little he has prepared the way for his masterpiece of deception in the development of spiritualism.[399]

My friend, the world is ripe for Satan's crowning act of deception! Through mass media, literature, public education, psychic phenomena, the paranormal, movies, environmental concerns, and various pagan practices, Satan is conditioning people for his master deception.

Knowing that there is precious little time left in this world's history, he has pulled out all the stops in his effort to condition minds and gain the allegiance of an entire generation of the human race through deceit, ignorance, and spiritualism.

The Three Frogs of Revelation

Revelation 16:13 describes three unclean spirits that look like frogs. They portray a trio of historical enemies of the church that at the end will attempt to deceive the whole world and war against the remnant. We have always been quick to identify the beast and the false prophet as papal Rome and apostate Protestantism. But what about the frog-like spirit that comes out of the "dragon?"

Dwight Nelson, while writing his book *Countdown to the Showdown,* was asked where he thought the eastern half of this globe fit into the apocalypse. His response was that they are represented as the first frog-like spirit that comes out of the dragon's mouth—"the New Age/Old Age of eastern mysticism, animism, and spiritism."[400] And he is right! Modern spiritualism/New Age will be the bonding that will unite Rome and Protestant America in the final conspiracy against the faithful.

> Through the two great errors, the immortality of the soul and Sunday sacredness, Satan will bring the people under his deceptions. While the former lays the foundation of spiritualism, the latter creates a bond of sympathy with Rome. The Protestants of the United States will be foremost in stretching their hands across the gulf to grasp the

hand of spiritualism; they will reach over the abyss to clasp hands with the Roman power; and under the influence of this threefold union, this country will follow in the steps of Rome in trampling on the rights of conscience.[401]

Scriptures safeguard against deception

One thing, however, is certain: Satan will not be permitted to counterfeit the manner of Christ's glorious second coming. The two-hundred plus biblical references to the second coming of Christ are in the Scriptures to safeguard us from Satan's counterfeit. God's Word teaches that Christ's second coming will be spectacular and world-wide. Let me share with you a few pronouncements on the Second Coming made by Jesus and other New Testament writers.

"For as the lightning cometh out of the east, and shineth even unto the west; so shall also the coming of the Son of man be" (Matt 24:27). Jesus will come "in the clouds of heaven with power and great glory" (Matt 24:30). "Every eye shall see him" (Rev. 1:7). There will be millions of bright angels accompanying Him (Jude 14). "The King of kings descends upon the cloud, wrapped in flaming fire. The heavens are rolled together as a scroll, the earth trembles before Him and every mountain and island is moved out of its place."[402]

This climactic event will be the ultimate, universal, most spectacular display of sight and sound that humans have ever experienced. No human mind can fully comprehend that scene. No human pen can portray that event. Even though Satan will not be able to enact the manner or the grandeur of the majestic second coming of Christ, he will succeed in deceiving millions of Christians and non-Christians alike.

That's why Jesus warned His followers, "If someone should say to you Jesus is at a certain place, don't you believe it. And if they tell you he's in a secret location, don't believe that either."

We've seen how both the Bible and the Spirit of Prophecy warn against the last great deception. We've seen how Satan is aggressively conditioning and preparing people for his crowning act of deception. We see the evidence all around us of modern spiritualism and how the world is ripe for the appearing of the false "christ." What can we do about it?

My friend, the only safeguard against this crowning act of deception is to study the Bible, know the truth for yourself, and pray for spiritual discernment. The servant of the Lord says: "Only those who have been diligent students of the Scripture and who have received the love of the truth will be shielded from the powerful delusion that takes the world captive."[403]

The members of the church who have been rooted and grounded in the truth will not be led astray by the New Age spirituality or any other wind of false doctrine. They will know their true Redeemer and will exclaim, "Lo, this is our God; we have waited for Him, and He will save us" (Isaiah 25:9) when they see Him appear in the clouds of glory.

Spiritualism in all its various forms, overt or subtle, is still Satan's most alluring, intriguing and deceptive weapon for the ruin of the human race. He deceived Eve with it and is seducing millions today. As we enter the last days of this world's history, let us pray most fervently for the Holy Spirit in our lives, for spiritual discernment and finally put on the whole armor of God "for we wrestle not against flesh and blood, but against principalities, against powers, against the rulers of the darkness of this world, against spiritual wickedness in high places" (Ephesians 6:12).

Endnotes

1 Richard N. Ostling, "One Nation Under Gods," (*Time*, Special Issue, Fall 1993), 62.

2 Ibid.

3 Russell Chandler, *Understanding the New Age* (Dallas: Word Publishing, 1988), 20.

4 Jerry Adler, "800,000 Hands Clapping," (*Newsweek*, June 13, 1994),46.

5 See Ellen G. White, *The Great Controversy Between Christ and Satan*, (Nampa, Idaho: Pacific Press, 1939), 551-553, and Lewis Spence, *Encyclopaedia of Occultism* (New Hyde Park, N.Y.: University Books, 1960), 381.

6 Bob Woodward, *The Choice* (New York: Simon & Schuster, 1996), 130.

7 Ellen G. White, *Patriarchs and Prophets* (Nampa, Idaho: Pacific Press, 1958), 688

8 Spence, *Encyclopaedia of Occultism*, 392.

9 J. Gordon Melton, Jerome Clark, and Aidan A. Kelly, *New Age Almanac* (Detroit: Visible Ink Press, 1991), 4.

10 Emanuel Swedenborg, *Concerning Heaven and Its Wonders, and Concerning Hell* (London: Otis Clapp, 1850), 64, 65.

11 Spence, *Encyclopaedia of Occultism*, 392-395.

12 Robert C. Fuller, *Alternative Medicine and American Religious Life* (New York: Oxford University Press, 1989), 49.

13 Fuller, *Alternative Medicine*, 49, 50.

14 Fuller, *Alternative Medicine*, 50.

15 Franz Anton Mesmer, *Mesmerism: A Translation of the Original Scientific and Medical Writings of F. A. Mesmer* (Los Altos, Calif.: William Kaufmann, 1980), 51.

[16] Fuller, *Alternative Medicine and American Religious Life*, 39.

[17] Melton, Clark, and Kelly, *New Age Almanac*, 5.

[18] Peter Washington, *Madame Blavatsky's Baboon* (New York: Schocken Books, 1995), 16.

[19] Fuller, *Alternative Medicine*, 51.

[20] "Emerson, Ralph Waldo," *The New Encyclopaedia Britannica* (1993 edition).

[21] J. D. Douglas, general editor, *The New International Dictionary of the Christian Church* (Grand Rapids: Zondervan Publishing House, 1978), 340.

[22] "Emerson, Ralph Waldo," *The New Encyclopaedia Britannica* (1993 edition).

[23] Ralph Waldo Emerson, *Self Reliance* (New York: Funk & Wagnalls, 1975), 17.

[24] Emerson, *Self Reliance*, 17.

[25] H. P. Blavatsky, *Isis Unveiled* (Wheaton: Theosophical Publishing House, 1972), xli.

[26] H. M. Kallen, "Theosophist," *The World Book Encyclopedia* (1973), 192.

[27] Melton, Clark, and Kelly, *New Age Almanac*, 16.

[28] Ibid., 16.

[29] Ibid., 14.

[30] Ibid., 7.

[31] Ibid., 11.

[32] Ibid., 10.

[33] White, *Great Controversy*, 553.

[34] Spence, *Encyclopaedia of Occultism*, 381.

[35] White, *Great Controversy*, 551.

[36] *This Fabulous Century,* 1960–1970 (USA: Time Life Books, 1988), 43.

[37] *Upbeat Magazine* 7 (December 1983): 23, quoted in Norman L. Geisler and J. Yutaka Amana, *The Reincarnation Sensation* (Wheaton: Tyndale House Publishers, 1986), 18.

[38] Ruth Montgomery and Joanne Garland, *Ruth Montgomery: Herald of the New Age* (Garden City, N.Y.: Doubleday & Company, Inc., 1986), 234.

[39] Melton, Clark, and Kelly, *New Age Almanac,* 169.

[40] Ibid., 174.

[41] John Naisbitt and Patricia Aburdene Naisbitt, *Megatrends 2000* (New York: William Morrow & Co., 1990), 133.

[42] Ibid., 134.

[43] Edward W. Campion, M.D., "Why Unconventional Medicine?" *New England Journal of Medicine* (January 1993): 282.

[44] Claudia Wallis, "Why New Age Medicine Is Catching On," *Time,* November 4, 1991, 68.

[45] Russell Chandler, *Understanding the New Age* (Dallas: Word Publishing, 1988), 163.

[46] Reisser, Reisser, and Weldon, *New Age Medicine,* 12.

[47] Fuller, *Alternative Medicine,* 3.

[48] Ted J. Kaptchuk, *Chinese Medicine: The Web That Has No Weaver* (London: Rider Books, 1983), 81, 83.

[49] Marilyn Ferguson, *The Aquarian Conspiracy* (Los Angeles, Calif.: J. P. Tarcher, Inc., 1980), 242.

[50] Paul C. Reisser, Teri K. Reisser, and John Weldon, *The Holistic Healers: A Christian Perspective on New Age Health Care* (Downers Grove: InterVarsity Press, 1983), 22.

[51] Ferguson, *Aquarian Conspiracy,* 257, 258.

[52] Arthur W. Hafner, Ph.D. Hafner, *Reader's Guide to Alternative Health Methods*

(Milwaukee, Wis.: American Medical Association, 1993), 325-338.

53 Reisser, Reisser, and Weldon, *New Age Medicine*, 10, 11.

54 Joel Stein, "The God Squad," *Time*, Sept. 22, 1997, 97.

55 Ibid., 100.

56 Ibid., 98-99.

57 *Break Point with Chuck Colson, No. 70926* (Washington, D.C.: Prison Fellowship Ministries, Sept. 26, 1997), page 1.

58 Chuck Norris, *The Secret Power Within: Zen Solutions to Real Problems* (New York: Little, Brown and Company, 1996), 36.

59 Patricia Lu Pillot, "Belt Rank." *Black Belt*, Nov, 1985, 63.

60 Melton, Clark, and Kelly, *New Age Almanac*, 335.

61 David Van Diema, "Buddhism in America? *Time*, Oct. 13, 1997, 74.

62 Ibid.

63 Gerald Clarke, "I've Got to Get My Life Back Again." *Time*, May 23, 1983.

64 "George Lucas Believes in the Force of Myths, Fairy Tales," interview with Joanne Waterman Williams. *Chicago Sun-Times*, May 18, 1980, as quoted in *The Gospel from Outer Space* by Robert Short (San Francisco: Harper & Row, Publishers, 1983), 49.

65 Ibid.

66 Bruce Handy, "The Force Is Back," *Time*, February 10, 1997, 74.

67 Betty Sue Flowers, editor, *The Power of Myth* (New York: Doubleday, 1988), 148.

68 Stephen and Robin Larsen, *A Fire in the Mind: The Life of Joseph Campbell* (New York: Doubleday, 1991), 106.

69 Alan MacDonald, *Movies in Close-Up* (Downers Grove: InterVarsity Press, 1992), 31, 32.

[70] Andy Mangels, *Star Wars, The Essential Guide to Characters* (New York: Ballantine Books, 1995), 191.

[71] Donald F. Glut, *Star Wars: The Empire Strikes Back* (New York: Ballantine Books, 1980), 120.

[72] Mangels, *Movies,* 191.

[73] George Ryley Scott, *Phallic Worship: A History of Sex & Sexual Rites* (London: Random House Publishers, 1966), 158.

[74] Vishal Mangalwadi, *When the New Age Gets Old: Looking for a Greater Spirituality* (Downers Grove: InterVarsity Press, 1992), 110.

[75] White, *Great Controversy,* 555.

[76] Ferguson, *Aquarian Conspiracy,* 280.

[77] Ibid.

[78] Ibid., 281.

[79] Ibid., 315.

[80] Ibid., 295.

[81] Ellen G. White, *Education* (Nampa, Idaho: Pacific Press, 1952), 13.

[82] John Ankerberg & Craig Branch, *Thieves of Innocence* (Eugene, Ore.: Harvest House Publishers, 1993),8.

[83] Ferguson, *The Aquarian Conspiracy,*287.

[84] Eric Buehrer, *The New Age Masquerade* (Brentwood, Tenn.: Wolgemuth & Hyatt, Publishers, Inc., 1990), 42

[85] Buehrer, *The New Age Masquerade,* 33, 34.

[86] John Ankerberg and John Weldon, *Encyclopedia of New Age Beliefs* (Eugene, Ore.: Harvest House Publishers, 1996),416.

[87] Ibid., 426.

[88] Ibid., 426, 427.

[89] Quoted in *Encyclopedia of New Age Beliefs*, 426.

[90] Melton, Clark, and Kelly, *New Age Almanac* (New York: Visible Ink Press, 1991), 409.

[91] Jean Houston, *A Mythic Life* (New York: HarperCollins Publishers, 1996), 169.

[92] Melton, Clark, and Kelly, *New Age Almanac*, 409.

[93] David B. Ellis, *Becoming a Master Student*, 5th ed. (Rapid City, S. Dak.: College Survival, Inc., 1985), 78.

[94] Ibid., 234.

[95] Ibid., 234.

[96] Rosemary Ellen Guiley, *Harper's Encyclopedia of Mystical & Personal Experience* (New York: HarperCollins Publishers, 1991), 412.

[97] Ellis, *Becoming a Master Student*, 234.

[98] White, *Education*, 13.

[99] Ellen G. White, *Counsels to Parents, Teachers and Students* (Nampa, Idaho: Pacific Press, 1943), 66.

[100] Geoffrey Giuliano, *The Lost Beatles Interviews* (New York: Penguin Books USA, Inc., 1994), 114, 114o.

[101] Giuliano, *Lost Beatles Interviews*, 98

[102] Giuliano, *Lost Beatles Interviews*, 107.

[103] *Upbeat Magazine*: 7 (December, 1983).

[104] Giuliano, *Lost Beatles Interviews* 129, 130.

[105] *The John Lennon Collection* (of sheet music) (Milwaukee, Wis.: Hal Leonard Publishing Corporation, 1983), 38-40.

[106] Giuliano, *Lost Beatles Interviews*, 337, 338.

[107] Larson, *Larson's Book of Rock*, 46.

[108] Guiliano, *The Lost Beatles Interviews*, 375, 377.

[109] Guiliano, *The Lost Beatles Interviews*, 369.

[110] *Dupree's Diamond News*, Issue No. 35, Fall, 1996, 1.

[111] Caryl Matriciana, *Gods of the New Age* (Eugene, Ore.: Harvest House Publishers, 1985), 11.

[112] Ibid., 13.

[113] Ibid., 14.

[114] Bob Larson, *Larson's Book of Rock* (Wheaton: Tyndale House Publishers, Inc., 1987), 145.

[115] Bob Larson, *Larson's Book of Rock* (Wheaton: Tyndale House Publishers, Inc., 1987), 178.

[116] Alan Menken and Stephen Schwartz, "Colors of the Wind" from Pocahontas (Wonderland Music Company, Inc., and Walt Disney Music Company, 1995).

[117] Melton, Clark, and Kelly, *New Age Almanac*, 73.

[118] Douglas Groothuis, *Confronting the New Age* (Downers Grove: InverVarsity Press, 1988), 190-192.

[119] Melton, Clark, and Kelly, *New Age Almanac*, 77.

[120] Groothuis, *Confronting the New Age*, 192.

[121] Gerri Hirshey, "Acropolis Now" (*GQ Magazine*, Vol. 65, Number 5, May, 1995), 168-170.

[122] *Los Angeles Times* Business Section, July 4, 1995.

[123] *Shakti*, with John McLaughlin album cover notes (Sony Music Entertainment Inc/Manufactured by Columbia Records, New York, 1991), 4.

[124] *Enigma*, MCMXC A. D., (Sweet "N" Sour Songs, Ltd., Virgin Music, Inc. ASCAP)

[125] H. Wayne House, "Traveling Down the Road Less Traveled." *Christian Research Journal,* Spring, 1996, 29.

[126] M. Scott Peck, *Further Along the Road Less Traveled* (New York: Simon & Schuster, 1993), 156-7.

[127] Ibid.,156.

[128] Ibid., 155.

[129] House, "Traveling Down the Road Less Traveled." 29.

[130] M. Scott Peck, *The Road Less Traveled* (New York: Simon and Schuster, 1978), 74.

[131] Peck, *The Road Less Traveled,* 76.

[132] Ibid., 270.

[133] Ibid., 271-273.

[134] Ibid., 281.

[135] M. Scott Peck, *The Different Drum: Community Making and Peace* (New York: Simon & Schuster, 1987), 17.

[136] Ibid., 21.

[137] Rosemary Ellen Guiley, *Harper's Encyclopedia of Mystical & Paranormal Experience* (New York: HarperCollins Publishers, 1991),556.

[138] Ankeberg and Weldon, *Encyclopedia of New Age Beliefs,* 200.

[139] Richard J. Foster, *Richard J. Foster's Study Guide for Celebration of Discipline* (San Francisco: Harper & Row, Publishers, 1983), 22.

[140] Guiley, *Harper's Encyclopedia of Mystical & Paranormal Experience.* 485.

[141] Ankerberg and Weldon, *Encyclopedia of New Age Beliefs.* 416.

[142] Richard J. Foster, *Celebration of Discipline: The Path to Spiritual Growth* (San Francisco: Harper & Row, Publishers, 1978), 21.

[143] Ibid., 26.

[144] Ankerberg and Weldon, *Encyclopedia of New Age Beliefs,* 461.

[145] Will Baron, *Deceived by the New Age* (Boise, Idaho: Pacific Press, 1990), 61-71.

[146] Letter to Will Baron from Summer, June 12, 1992.

[147] Foster, *Celebration of Discipline,* (1978 edition), 27.

[148] *Christian Research Institute International,* "Richard Foster/Celebration of Discipline." Statement No. 3:062. May 3, 1996.

[149] Shirley MacLaine, *Out on a Limb* (New York: Bantam Books, 1984), 327, 328.

[150] Ibid., 329.

[151] Mary Shrode, *Just Imagine With Barney* (Allen: The Lyons Group, 1992), 8.

[152] Ibid.,18.

[153] MacLaine, *Out on a Limb*, 327.

[154] Ibid., 329.

[155] Ellen G. White, *Selected Messages,* Book 3 (Hagerstown, Md.: Review & Herald, 1980), 36, 37.

[156] Guiley, *Harper's Encyclopedia,* 420.

[157] Laurie Beth Jones, *The Path: Creating Your Mission Statement for Work and for Life (*New York: Hyperion, 1996), 42.

[158] Laurie Beth Jones, *Jesus: CEO: Using Ancient Wisdom for Visionary Leadership* (New York: Hyperion, 1995), 13.

[159] Ibid., 17.

[160] Wendy Kaminer, "Why We Love Gurus," *Time* Oct. 20, 1997, 60.

[161] Elisabeth Sahtouris, PhD., *Gaia, The Human Journey From Chaos to Cosmos,* (New York: Pocket books, 1989), 21-23.

[162] Carol J. Adams, *Ecofeminism and the Sacred.* New York: Continuum Publishing Company, 1993), 13.

[163] Al Gore, *Earth in the Balance, Ecology and the Human Spirit* (Boston, Mass.: Houghton MifflinCompany, 1992), 1.

[164] Ibid., 258, 259.

[165] Tony Campolo, *How to Rescue the Earth Without Worshiping Nature* (Nashville, Tenn.: Thomas Nelson, Publishers, 1992), 173-174.

[166] John Harvey Kellogg, *The Living Temple* (Battle Creek, Mich.: Good Health Publishing Company, 1903), 29.

[167] Ellen G. White, *Medical Ministry* (Nampa, Idaho: Pacific Press, 1963) 98.

[168] Patricia Aberdeen, *Megatrends for Women* (New York: Villard Books, 1992), 108, 109.

[169] Ibid., 112, 113.

[170] Ibid., 244.

[171] Widgelman with Nikkifinke Greenberg, "The Megatrends Man," *Newsweek,* September 23, 1985, 61.

[172] Cynthia Eller, *Living in the Lap of the Goddess* (New York: Crossroad Publishing Company, 1993), 18.

[173] *Premier Magazine,* July, 1995, 82.

[174] *Time,* July 19, 1995.

[175] Frances Mossiker, *Pocahontas, The Life and Legend* (New York: Alfred A. Knopf, 1976), 38

[176] E. Adamson Hoebel, "Pocahontas." *The World Book Encyclopedia* (Chicago: Field Enterprises Educational Corporation, 1973), 525.

[177] Nancy Gibbs, "Angels Among Us." *Time,* December 27, 1993, 56.

[178] Ibid.

[179] Ankerberg and Weldon, *Encyclopedia of New Age Beliefs,* 28.

[180] Nancy Gibbs, "Angels Among Us," 58.

[181] Ellen G. White, *Selected Messages,* Book 2 (Hagerstown, Md.: Review

and Herald, 1986), 141,142.

[182] Ellen G. White, *Evangelism* (Hegerstown, Md.: Review and Herald, 1946), 589.

[183] Elizabeth Clare Prophet, *Angels, Angels, Angels* (Livingston, Mont.: Summit University Press), 12.

[184] Ibid., 18.

[185] (No author listed) *Profile: Elizabeth Clare Prophet* (Livingston, Mont.: Summit University Press), 8.

[186] Ibid., 2.

[187] Ibid., 7.

[188] Ibid., 2.

[189] Ibid., 7.

[190] White, *Great Controversy,* 513.

[191] Ibid., 516.

[192] Ibid., 517.

[193] Roger Morneau, *Beware of Angels* (Hagerstown, Md.: Review & Herald, 1997), 13-21.

[194] "Angel." *Seventh-day Adventist Dictionary,* Vol. 8 (Hagerstown, Md.: Review & Herald, 1960) 44.

[195] "The third part." (Revelation 12:4) *Seventh-day Adventist Bible Commentary,* Vol. 7 (Hagerstown, Md.: Review & Herald, 1960), 808

[196] Ellen G. White, "The Observance of Sabbath," *Testimonies for the Church,* Vol. 6 (Nampa, Idaho: Pacific Press, 1948), 366, 367.

[197] White, *Great Controversy,* 512, 513.

[198] Ibid., 513

[199] Ellen G. White, *The Desire of Ages* (Nampa, Idaho: Pacific Press Publishing Association, 1940), 369.

[200] Ellen G. White, *The Truth About Angels* (Nampa, Idaho: Pacific Press, 1996), 19.

[201] White, *Great Controversy*, 553.

[202] White, *Truth About Angels*, 262.

[203] Ellen G. White, *Early Writings*, (Hagerstown, Md.: Review and Herald, 1945), 262.

[204] Naisbitt and Naisbitt, *Megatrends 2000*, 133.

[205] Ibid., 134.

[206] Claudia Wallis, "Why New Age Medicine Is Catching On," *Time*, November 4, 1991, 68.

[207] David Van Biema, "Emperor of the Soul," *Time*, June 24, 1996, 65.

[208] Andrew Weil, *Spontaneous Healing*, (New York: Fawcett Columbine, 1995), 11.

[209] *Time* cover, May 12, 1997.

[210] Jeffrey Kluger, "Mr Natural," *Time*, May 12, 1997, 71.

[211] Jan Goodwin, "A Health Insurance Revolution," *New Age Journal*, 1997-1998 Special Edition, 67, 68.

[212] Ibid., 66.

[213] Reisser, Reisser, and Weldon, *The Holistic Healers*, 11.

[214] Ibid., 174.

[215] Paul C. Reisser, M.D., "Body, Mind & Soul: What Are Holistic Healers Really After?" *Journal of Christian Nursing* (Spring 1989). p. 10.

[216] Arthur W. Hafner, ed. *Reader's Guide to Alternative Health Methods* (Milwaukee, Wis.: American Medical Society, 1993), 104.

[217] Melton, Clark, and Kelly, *New Age Almanac*, 169.

[218] Ferguson, *Aquarian Conspiracy*, 257.

[219] Ibid., 257, 258.

[220] Baron, *Deceived by the New Age*, 13.

[221] Ibid., 25.

[222] Ibid., 26.

[223] Ibid., 25, 26.

[224] Ferguson, *Aquarian Conspiracy*, 26.

[225] Paul C. Reisser, Teri K. Reisser, and John Weldon, *New Age Medicine: A Christian Perspective on Holistic Health* (Downers Grove: InterVarsity Press, 1987), 12.

[226] White, *Evangelism*, 549.

[227] J. A. English-Lueck, *The Roots of Holistic Health* (Albuquerque, N. Mex.: University of New Mexico Press, 1990), 67.

[228] Ibid., 63.

[229] Ibid., 63

[230] Ferguson, *Aquarian Conspiracy*, 243.

[231] English-Lueck, *Roots of Holistic Health*, 69.

[232] Reisser, Reisser, and Weldon, *New Age Medicine*, 54.

[233] Ibid.

[234] Tom Monte and the editors of EastWest Natural Health, *World Medicine: The East West Guide to Healing Your Body* (New York: Putnam Publishing Group, 1993), 20.

[235] Ibid., 14.

[236] Xie Zhu-Fan, M.D., *Best of Traditional Chinese Medicine* (Beijing, China: New World Press, 1995), 1.

[237] Ibid., 2.

[238] Reisser, Reisser, and Weldon, *New Age Medicine*, 63.

[239] Ibid., 64.

[240] Ibid., 65.

[241] John Ankerberg and John Weldon, *Can You Trust Your Doctor?: The Complete Guide to New Age Medicine and Its Threats to Your Family* (Brentwood, Tenn.: Wolgemuth and Hyatt, Publishers, 1991), 109, 110.

[242] Xie, *Traditional Chinese Medicine*, 106.

[243] Cheng Xinnong, chief editor, *Chinese Acupuncture and Moxibustion* (Beijing, China: Foreign Languages Press, 1990), 339.

[244] Monte, *World Medicine*, 23.

[245] Ankerberg and Weldon, *Can You Trust Your Doctor?*, 109, 110.

[246] Hafner, *Reader's Guide to Alternative Health Methods*, 43.

[247] Cheng, *Chinese Acupuncture and Moxibustion*, 15.

[248] Xie, *Traditional Chinese Medicine*, 10.

[249] Cheng, *Chinese Acupuncture and Moxibustion*, 46.

[250] Elaine Liechti, *Shiatsu: Japanese Massage for Health and Fitness* (Rockport, Mass.: Element Books, 1992), 28.

[251] Ibid.

[252] Ibid.

[253] Cheng, *Traditional Chinese Medicine*, 10.

[254] MacLaine, *Out on a Limb*, 199, 200.

[255] Liechti, *Shiatsu*, 28.

[256] Monte, *World Medicine*, 26.

[257] Ibid., 246, 247.

[258] Pedro Chan, *Finger Acupressure* (New York: Ballantine Books, 1975), 11.

[259] Liechti, *Shiatsu,* 1.

[260] Monte, *World Medicine,* 247.

[261] Ibid., 74.

[262] Ibid., 75.

[263] Felix Mann, *The Meridians of Acupuncture* (London: William Heinemann Medical Books, 1964), 13.

[264] Peter Yuen, Acupuncturist and Director of the Loma Linda Pain Management Center, Loma Linda, California, telephone interview by author, July 2, 1996.

[265] Spence, *Encyclopaedia of Occultism,* 105.

[266] Will Baron, telephone interview by author, June 4, 1996.

[267] Frena Bloomfield, *Chinese Beliefs* (London: Arrow Books, 1986), 36.

[268] Ibid., 25.

[269] Ibid., 7.

[270] Reisser, Reisser, and Weldon, *New Age Medicine,* 34.

[271] Melton, Clark, and Kelly, *New Age Almanac,* 5.

[272] Fuller, *Alternative Medicine,* 71.

[273] George Vithoulkas, *Homeopathy: Medicine of the New Man* (New York: Prentice Hall Press, 1987), 6.

[274] Spence, *Encyclopaedia of Occultism,* 142.

[275] Reisser, Reisser, and Weldon, *New Age Medicine,* 34.

[276] Ibid.

[277] Ellen G. White, *Conflict and Courage* (Hagerstown, Md.: Review and Herald, 1970), 21.

[278] John Diamond, M.D., *BK: Behavioral Kinesiology* (New York: Harper & Row, Publishers, 1979), 6.

[279] Ankerberg and Weldon, *Can You Trust Your Doctor?* p. 158.

[280] Hafner, *Reader's Guide to Alternative Health Methods*, 208.

[281] Ankerberg and Weldon, *Can You Trust Your Doctor?* p. 28.

[282] Ibid., 28

[283] Ibid., 49.

[284] Ibid., 28.

[285] Ibid., 7.

[286] Deepak Chopra, M.D., *Quantum Healing: Exploring the Frontiers of Mind/Body Medicine* (New York: Bantam Books, 1989), 5.

[287] Scott Gerson, M.D., *Ayurveda: The Ancient Indian Healing Art* (Rockport, Mass.: Element Books, 1993), 3.

[288] Ibid.

[289] Monte, *World Medicine*, 30.

[290] Gerson, *Ayurveda*, 85.

[291] David Van Biema, "Emperor of the Soul," *Time*, June 24, 1996, 67.

[292] Ibid., 66.

[293] Williams, *New Age Healing*, 76.

[294] Burton Goldberg Group, *Alternative Medicine: The Definitive Guide* (Fife, Wash.: Burton Goldberg Group, 1995), 63.

[295] Ibid., 65.

[296] Gerson, *Ayurveda*, 53.

[297] Gerson, *Ayurveda*, 5.

[298] Van Biema, "Emperor of the Soul," 68.

[299] Burton Goldberg group, *Alternative Medicine*, 340, 341.

[300] Burton Goldberg group, *Alternative Medicine*, 341.

[301] John B. Noss, *Man's Religions*, 5th ed. (New York: Macmillan Publishing Co., 1974), 197-198.

[302] Melton, Clark, and Kelly, *New Age Almanac*, 147.

[303] Jack Raso, *"Alternative" Healthcare: A Comprehensive Guide* (Amherst, N. Y.: Prometheus Books, 1994), 54.

[304] Melton, Clark, and Kelly, *New Age Almanac*, 150.

[305] Melton, Clark, and Kelly, *New Age Almanac*, 151.

[306] Monte, *World Medicine*, 168.

[307] Matrisciana, *Gods of the New Age*, 144.

[308] Morton T. Kelsey, *The Other Side of Silence: A Guide to Christian Meditation* (New York: Paulist Press, 1976), 179.

[309] Ibid., 70, 71.

[310] Gopi Krishna, *Living with Kundalini* (Boston: Shambhala, 1993), 143.

[311] John Ankerberg and John Weldon, *The Facts on Holistic Health and the New Medicine* (Eugene, Ore.: Harvest House Publishers, 1992), 37.

[312] C. Norman Shealy, M.D., Ph.D., *Occult Medicine Can Save Your Life: A Modern Doctor Looks at Unconventional Healing* (Columbia, Ohio: Brindabella Books, 1985), 153.

[313] Ibid., 166.

[314] Williams, *New Age Healing*, 94.

[315] Ibid., 94.

[316] *Webster's New World Dictionary*, 2d college ed (1982), s.v. "Mandala."

[317] Marvin Karlins and Lewis M. Andrews, *Biofeedback: Turning on the Power of Your Mind* (New York: Warner Communications Co., 1974), 71, 72.

[318] Hafner, *Reader's Guide to Alternative Health Methods*, 279.

[319] Shirley Lord, ed., "Holistic Treatments," *Vogue Beauty,* December 1991, 172.

[320] Hafner, *Reader's Guide to Alternative Health Methods,* 279.

[321] Vithoulkas, *Homeopathy, Medicine of the New Man,* 6.

[322] Margot McCarthy, ed., *Natural Therapies* (San Francisco, Calif.: Harper Collins Publishers, 1994), 149.

[323] Vithoulkas, *Homeopathy: Medicine of the New Man,* 21.

[324] Ibid.

[325] Hafner, *Reader's Guide to Alternative Health Methods,* 85.

[326] Raso, *"Alternative" Healthcare,* 139.

[327] *Organon of Medicine,* 6th ed., (New Delhi, India: B. Jain Publishers, 1978), 17, 18, quoted in Ankerberg and Weldon, *Can You Trust Your Doctor?,* 270.

[328] Dolores Krieger, Ph.D., R.N., *The Therapeutic Touch: How to Use Your Hands to Help or Heal* (New York: A Fireside Book, 1979), 11-16.

[329] David Sneed and Sharon Sneed, *The Hidden Agenda: A Critical View of Alternative Medical Therapies,* (Nashville: Thomas Nelson, 1991), 168.

[330] Sharon Fish, "'Therapeutic Touch': Healing Science or Psychic Midwife?" *Christian Research Journal* (Summer 1995), 30.

[331] Krieger, *The Therapeutic Touch,* 35.

[332] Ibid.

[333] Ibid.

[334] Ibid., 36.

[335] Ibid.

[336] Ibid., 71.

[337] Joe Maxwell, "Nursing's New Age?" *Christianity Today,* February 5, 1996, 96.

[338] Steve Barrett and William T. Jarvis, *The Health Robbers: A Close Look at Quackery in America* (Buffalo, N. Y.: Prometheus Books, 1993), 364.

[339] Williams, *New Age Healing*, 128.

[340] Hafner, *Reader's Guide to Alternative Health Methods*, 94.

[341] Marianne Uhl, *Chakra Energy Massage* (Wilmot, Wis.: Lotus Light Publications, 1988), 100,101.

[342] Raso, *"Alternative" Healthcare*, 197.

[343] Barrett and Jarvis, ed. The Health Robbers, 361.

[344] Warren Peters, *Mystical Medicine* (Rapidan, Va.: Hartland Publications, 1988), 50.

[345] Uhl, *Chakra Energy Massage*, 15.

[346] Ankerberg and Weldon, *The Facts on Holistic Health and the New Medicine*, 41.

[347] Melton, Clark, and Kelly, *New Age Almanac*, 242.

[348] Maybelle Segal, *Reflexology* (Hollywood, Calif.: Melvin Powers Wilshire Book Co., 1976), 16.

[349] Ibid.

[350] Williams, *New Age Healing*, 22.

[351] Ibid., 78.

[352] Greg Nielsen, *Beyond Pendulum Power: Entering the Energy World* (Reno, Nev.: Conscious Books, 1988), 5.

[353] D. Jurriaanse, *The Practical Pendulum Book* (York Beach, Maine: Samuel Weiser, 1986), 1.

[354] Nielsen, *Beyond Pendulum Power*, i.

[355] Williams, *New Age Healing*, 38.

[356] Samuel Pfeifer, *Healing at Any Price?* (Milton Keynes, England: Word Limited, 1988), 68, quoted in Ankerberg and Weldon, *Can You Trust Your Doctor?*, 317.

[357] Richard Williams, senior editor, *New Age Healing.* (Pleasantville, N. Y.: Reader's Digest Association, Inc., 1992), 55.

[358] Ibid.

[359] Melton, Clark, and Kelly, *New Age Almanac,* 344.

[360] Thomas Sugrue, *The Story of Edgar Cayce* (New York: Dell Publishing Co., 1967), 5.

[361] Sugrue, *The Story of Edgar Cayce,* 109.

[362] Ankerberg and Weldon, *Can You Trust Your Doctor?*, 342, 343.

[363] Melton, Clark, and Kelly, *New Age Almanac,* 179.

[364] Ankerberg and Weldon, *Can You Trust Your Doctor?*, 85.

[365] Ibid., 329.

[366] Melton, Clark, and Kelly, *New Age Almanac,* 31.

[367] C. Norman Shealy, *Occult Medicine Can Save Your Life* (Columbus, Ohio: Brindabella Books, 1985), 83.

[368] Elmer Green and Alyce Green, *Beyond Biofeedback* (Ft. Wayne, Ind.: Knoll Publishing Co., 1977), 13.

[369] Ibid., 344, 345.

[370] Ibid., 290.

[371] Maxwell, "Nursing's New Age," 96.

[372] Krieger, *The Therapeutic Touch,* 11-16.

[373] Raso, *"Alternative" Healthcare*, 229.

[374] Krieger, *The Therapeutic Touch,* 4.

[375] Maxwell, "Nursing's New Age," 96.

[376] John E. Smith, "William James" *World Book Encyclopedia*, Vol. 11

(Chicago: Field Enterprises Educational Corporation, 1973) 25.

[377] Biblical Research Institute, *The New Age Movement and Seventh-day Adventists*, 25.

[378] *Webster's New World Dictionary*, 2d college ed. (1984), s.v. "Placebo."

[379] Williams, *New Age Healing*, 46.

[380] Biblical Research Institute, *The New Age Movement* 12.

[381] Jochen Hawlischek, "Natural Medicine," May 1991, TMs, 2.

[382] Biblical Research Institute, 14, 15.

[383] Leslie Hardinge and Frank Holbrook, "Holiness and the Dark Powers," *Adult Sabbath School Lesson Quarterly*, January-March, 1989, 65.

[384] Albert Whiting, "Alternative Forms of Treatment," TMs, 2.

[385] William G. Johnsson, "Kellogg Revisited." *Adventist Review*, October 13, 1994, 4.

[386] Roger Coon, "Paulson Articles and Misc." White Estate Document File #269 GSEM 534.5.

[387] White, *Evangelism*, 606-609.

[388] Ibid., 606.

[389] Ellen G. White, *The Ministry of Healing* (Nampa, Idaho: Pacific Press, 1942), 127.

[390] Biblical Research Institute, *The New Age Movement*, 23.

[391] Biblical Research Institute, *The New Age Movement*, 14.

[392] White, *Great Controversy*, 624.

[393] Ellen G. White, *Last Day Events* (Nampa, Idaho: Pacific Press, 1992), 166.

[394] Ellen G. White, *Counsels on Health* (Nampa, Idaho: Pacific Press, 1951), 460.

[395] White, *Great Controversy*, 560.

[396] White, *Great Controversy*, 559.

[397] White, *Christ's Object Lessons*, 415.

[398] White, *Great Controversy*, 624.

[399] White, *Great Controversy*, 561.

[400] Dwight Nelson, *Countdown to the Showdown* (Fallbrook, Calif.: HART Research Center, 1992), 94.

[401] White, *Great Controversy*, 588.

[402] White, *Great Controversy*, 641, 642.

[403] White, *Great Controversy*, 625.